SINGLE
AND
FORCED
TO
MINGLE

SINGLE

AND

FORCED

TO

MINGLE

A Guide for (Nearly) Any Socially Awkward Situation

MELISSA CROCE

ATRIA BOOKS

New York   London   Toronto   Sydney   New Delhi

ATRIA
BOOKS

An Imprint of Simon & Schuster, Inc.
1230 Avenue of the Americas
New York, NY 10020

First Atria Books hardcover edition January 2021

ATRIA B O O K S and colophon are trademarks
of Simon & Schuster, Inc.

For information about special discounts for bulk purchases,
please contact Simon & Schuster Special Sales at 1-866-506-1949
or business@simonandschuster.com.

The Simon & Schuster Speakers Bureau can bring authors to
your live event. For more information or to book an event, contact
the Simon & Schuster Speakers Bureau at 1-866-248-3049
or visit our website at www.simonspeakers.com.

Manufactured in the United States of America

1   3   5   7   9   10   8   6   4   2

Library of Congress Cataloging-in-Publication Data

Names: Croce, Melissa, author.
Title: Single and forced to mingle : a guide for (nearly) any
socially awkward situation / Melissa Croce.
Description: First Atria Books hardcover edition. | New York : Atria Books,
2020. | Summary: "A laugh-out-loud, tongue-in-cheek guidebook filled
with hilarious and helpful advice-from how to dodge family members'
unwanted questions about babies to successfully creating a fake partner
during wedding season-for anyone trying to survive and thrive in the
midst of singledom"—Provided by publisher.
Identifiers: LCCN 2020033733 (print) | LCCN 2020033734 (ebook) |
ISBN 9781982144340 (hardcover) | ISBN 9781982144357 (ebook)
Subjects: LCSH: Single people—Life skills guides. | Single people—
Humor. | Interpersonal relations.
Classification: LCC HQ800 .C888 2020 (print) | LCC HQ800
(ebook) | DDC 646.7/0086/52—dc23
LC record available at https://lccn.loc.gov/2020033733
LC ebook record available at https://lccn.loc.gov/2020033734

ISBN 978-1-9821-4434-0
ISBN 978-1-9821-4435-7 (ebook)

To my mom, Chris, who is one of
the very few people in my life who has
never once asked me about my dating life.
That is just the cherry on top of all of the many
things that I love and appreciate about you.

Contents

CONTENTS

Foreword

So, you're single. That's why you're reading this book, right? (I'm not saying that if you're in a relationship you can't read this, but also, why would you want to??) Whether you're newly single or have been on this solo journey for a while, I'm glad you're here! Really. After a couple of long-term relationships, I found myself single for the first time in a while, and I soon realized, after the heartache faded, that the fact of the matter is this: Being. Single. Is. Awesome. It's been a few years since that epiphany and I've been single ever since, 100 percent by choice. I'm sure there are some of you reading this who think I'm full of shit, but hopefully some of you are also thinking, *Girl, same*, or even, *Thank God I'm not the only one who feels this way.*

A couple of years ago, I jokingly made a brochure to hand out to relatives at my cousin's wedding that included a snarky "choose your own adventure"–type chart about why I was single, and it went viral on Twitter. What really surprised me, though, were the responses: across gender, sexual orientation, culture, and religion, people felt the same way I did: dread at navigating social events as a single person. Not only was I not the only person to feel this way, but, in an era in which people are marrying much later in life, if at all, there were actually quite a lot of us! Being single is normal, *common*, and not an indicator of something being Wrong with us.

Maybe you don't want to be single (which is a totally valid stance!). Maybe you do want to be single because you're focused on other things, or are aro and/or ace and don't want to have any romantic or sexual relationships, or maybe you're just like me, and are perfectly happy Doing Life on your own (also all valid!). But regardless of how you feel about your Single Status, there are a lot of people out there—your mom, your (married) best friend, your aunt Carol, society—who might make you feel bad about it, whether they mean to or not. To them, being single isn't something to aspire to or be content with, it's something to be avoided, and that can make interacting with those people Annoying, to put it mildly. And as much as you might want to, you can't avoid all of those people (or society) forever.

Enter: *Single and Forced to Mingle.* Part semiserious how-to guide and part commiserator-in-crime, *Single and Forced to Mingle* is (meant to be) a humorous look at the life of a single millennial, including: giving tips on how to graciously endure the various scenarios in which single people find themselves (awkward small talk with an ex, navigating well-meaning but insensitive relatives at a wedding, and many more); what every newly single person needs to know; and arguments about why, actually, being single is really freaking awesome.

No matter how you may feel about Singledom, this book is for all of us. As I said before, being Single is the best.

Even if you don't believe me now, I hope by the end of the book, you do! (Or at the very least, you can pass this along to your aunt Carol, who will read it and hopefully stop making comments on when you're going to settle down and pop out babies!)

Good luck,
Melissa

I.

Singledom: A Starter Pack

Think of being a single person in the world as a hero going out on a long journey. There are things that one needs in order to successfully survive relatively unscathed in this dark world of meddling relatives and constant, excessive PDA by couples everywhere. But stick with me, and I'll show you how to not only survive but thrive!

THE QUINTESSENTIAL WARDROBE OF A SINGLE PERSON WHO IS FORCED TO MINGLE

- **Sunglasses.** This doesn't apply if it's dark or you're inside, because you're not a dick, but if you have to mingle at something like an outdoor wedding or pre-sunset happy hour, sunglasses are great armor—the more darkly tinted the better! If they're completely opaque, you can feel free to roll your eyes to your heart's content at whatever ridiculous sentence second cousin Randy had the nerve to utter.
- **Stunning Jewelry and/or Watch:** The tactic of wearing something ranging from merely eye-catching to outrageously gaudy will guarantee that at least one person, if not more than a few, will comment on this showstopping accessory, and thus perhaps won't ask you (at least immediately) about your love life. (You can also take this time to make up an outlandish tale about how you acquired said accessory, which could be fun and help pass the time.)
- **An Oldie but Goodie Wardrobe Staple:** Now is not the time to be a showstopper, no matter how tempting. *Do not* do Rent the Runway or order a new Stitch

Fix box, because even if you impress these people with whatever you get, you probably won't feel very comfortable wearing it. New clothes can be exciting, but nothing beats wearing your favorite outfit that you know looks good on you. You know the one—you always receive compliments when you wear it; it doesn't pull or tug or stretch in any way you don't want it to; and best of all, it's an outfit that doesn't make you look good, it looks good because you're wearing it.

- **Comfortable Shoes:** Obviously they need to go with your outfit and be appropriate for the occasion, but make 'em as comfortable as you can get away with. The reasoning is simple: so you can hightail it out of there as quickly as you can.

- **A Purse with the Works:** For anyone who presents traditionally as feminine, you probably know exactly what is meant by this. For anyone who presents traditionally as masculine, I suggest you flush any toxic masculinity down the toilet and get yourself a backpack, messenger bag, fanny pack, or honestly, a fantastic clutch, because you know what helps sell a lie besides sticking as close to the truth as possible? *Props.* And having a little travel bottle of Advil or Tums or Tylenol on you to wave around as you tell your boss that you don't feel well, and whatever you took isn't working, will come in handy. *Oh, look!* people will think. *They genuinely tried to stay longer. How thoughtful.* But they'll also be thinking that they don't want to catch whatever you have, and that it's best if you go home, honey, and rest. Right now. *Oh, darn, sorry you couldn't stay longer!!*

A SINGLE PERSON'S CALENDAR: EVERYTHING YOU NEED TO KNOW (AND STEER CLEAR OF!)

SUN	MON	TUES	WED	THURS	FRI	SAT
	1	✗	3	4	5	6
(7)	8	9	10	11	12	13
14	15	16	17	(18)	19	20
21	22	23	24	25	✗	27
28	(29)	30	31			

NOTES:
Call Mom!
Buy b-day gift
for Aunt Carol—
don't forget!!
Grocery list:
cheese, bread,
wine, vegetables(?)
Delete Tinder!
Change Netflix
password so ex
can't access!

Time marches forward, usually at a pace we can never quite seem to match, or are out of rhythm with. One minute you're sweating profusely, trying to eat all of your ice cream before it melts in the heat, the next you're hanging mostly functional twinkly lights around a frost-tinted window. Where does it go? Who can say? This book only deals with being single, not answering existential questions, sorry! But what it *can* do is give you a rundown of dates to keep on your calendar, so when you do come out of a life-induced haze, you'll be prepared for such monstrosities as Kiss a Ginger Day (January 12) or Reconciliation Day (April 2).

Means *STEER CLEAR OF!!!*

This section will be divided into seasons that people in relationships have *sigh* forced us to notice, whether we want to or not. And, of course, it doesn't follow a traditional calendar, so pay close attention!

CUFFING SEASON

Stretching from October to March, you'll be amazed at either the urge within yourself to couple up or to see it pop out in others who normally like to fly solo. The cold months and subdued energy of winter can make people susceptible to loneliness.

PROS:	CONS:
A good bed warmer and someone to kiss at midnight on New Year's Eve.	*Takes place during both the holiday season and Valentine's Day, and that can make a casual relationship feel a lot more serious than it is.*

October

❋ **03:** Boyfriend Day. Yes, this *should* be National *Mean Girls* Day, but I don't make the rules here. Stay off social media, for your own good.

November

• **11:** Singles Day. Hallelujah, our time has come! This "holiday" originated in China, namely as a shopping holiday specifically for bachelors, but the day has become more popular both with bachelorettes and in

Western society. One might be the loneliest number, but that doesn't mean you can't get great deals out of it.

- **30**: Personal Space Day. A godsend, especially between the Thanksgiving and winter holiday season. Take advantage of some peace and quiet!

December

TBH, all of this month is a Hazard to single people. Couples are constantly out and about, kissing under mistletoe, getting engaged over roaring fires, blah blah blah. If you have to go out into the world where romance lurks around every corner, I recommend always being slightly drunk on eggnog to make it bearable.

January

- **01**: Hangover Day/Bloody Mary Day. The only thing worse than New Year's Eve (you really would prefer to be at home than surrounded by people, and even worse is dealing with a crowd when you're all trying to go home at the same time, but societal expectations and FOMO make it near impossible to have a quiet night in. Maybe one day you'll be firm and just stay home, but this year is not the year.) is New Year's Day, and the inevitable hangover you have because you wanted to drink to forget you didn't have anyone to kiss at midnight. Your options are either to suffer with lots of water, Advil, and sleep, or do the hair of the dog and keep drinking right through it. Choices are good, right?

✹ **06**: Cuddle Day. You know what this means? Lots of PDA. Who knows how many couples observe this day, but you never know! It's good to always be prepared.

✹ **26**: Spouses Day. We get it, you're married; tell it to someone who cares. Next!

February

Now, maybe you might think that February is the worst month because it's very short, cold, and obsessed with romance. You're not wrong, but you also have the power to make this month into something more. There are apparently a lot of days dedicated to platonic friendship, and what's better than reminding your friends how grateful you are that you have them, at least?

- **07**: Send a Card to a Friend Day: Awwww!
- **11**: Make a Friend Day
- **13**: Galentine's Day
- ✹ **14**: Valentine's Day: I don't need to remind *you* of this horrendous holiday, but it bears repeating.
- **22**: Margarita Day: Oh, thank God.

SPRING FEVER

When Cuffing Season ends, Spring Fever begins, and lasts from March to June. Maybe you didn't participate in Cuffing Season, and now you're raring to go find a cute honey in the new sunshine. Or maybe you *did*, and you're feeling restless and tied down and you really would prefer to be flirtatious and free. Beware either way, because after Spring Fever ends, another dating season begins.

March

- **08:** International Women's Day
- **09:** Napping Day: Advocating for women's rights makes a bitch tired!
- **20:** Proposal Day: Not sure if all of the jewelry companies banded together at a recent conference to make this day an actual Thing, but beware of your Instagram feed and try not to go to any public sporting events. You never know what could happen.

April

- **11:** Pet Day: At least someone loves you!! Haha (oh, God, sigh). And your social media feeds will be filled with pictures of cute animals rather than humans. Always a plus.

May

- **11:** Eat What You Want Day: Anyone, single or not, can participate, obviously, but when society is telling you to "get fit" to "look hot" for the summer, give it the metaphorical middle finger and devour an entire sleeve of your Girl Scout cookie of choice.
- **25:** Wine Day: ROSÉ. ALL. DAY!!!!!!!!

SUMMER FLING

Lasting from Memorial Day to Labor Day, summer loving is a Thing, and if you don't believe me, ask John Travolta and Olivia Newton-John. Remember what I said about summertime being a season of more socialization and activity? Perhaps you feel compelled to have someone to take to all of those barbecues and rooftop happy hours. Some advice, though: if it's truly a fling, make sure you break up with them in that nebulous month of September, right before Cuffing Season starts back up again.

June

- **08**: Best Friends Day: Call your BFF up and tell them you love them!
- **09**: Sex Day: Calling all the freaky-deakies to get down on 6/9! Stay safe, use protection, practice verbal and enthusiastic consent, and have fun!

July

✺ **11**: Cheer Up the Lonely Day: Oh, God, can't you just *hear* Aunt Carol's voice as she pityingly calls to remind you that she loves you and also that time is ticking and "you don't want to die alone, do you, dear?" Don't pick up the phone today. Just don't do it. (You can call her back on July 26, which is Aunt and Uncle Day.)

August

- **10**: Lazy Day: Summer is a time of lots of socializing and mingling, so beg off today to be by yourself and chill out. Time to recharge!
- ✺ **25**: Kiss and Make Up Day: I know, you're probably like, "Why is there both a Reconciliation Day *and* a Kiss and Make Up Day?" I don't know, I'm just as baffled as you are! But keep an eye out for rose bouquet shortages and lots of overheard dramatic phone calls, especially if you regularly take public transportation.

✴ **31:** Matchmaker Day: Listen, if you want to have someone make you a match, find you a find, catch you a catch, then Godspeed and good luck to you, truly. But, if you can't take another botched attempt, then you know what to do: turn your phone off and don't answer any texts or calls until tomorrow.

CREATE YOUR PERFECT DATE AND WE'LL GIVE YOU A MILLENNIAL-APPROVED SOLITARY HOBBY TO TAKE UP

Create a "perfect date"—you chortle to yourself as you read this title. "Ha! I'll give you the perfect date." And then you proceed to think about that iconic line from the delightful movie *Miss Congeniality*—you know, the line about April 25. You feel clever! And you should, because it's a great line. But I'm calling your bluff here, because that's exactly the kind of date I want you to create. Surprise! (And don't pretend that you don't have an exact sort of weather, temperature, and humidity level you prefer. Even if you *think* you don't, you do.)

1. Pick your favorite season:
   a. Summer, obviously. Long days, balmy nights, cute clothes, what's not to love?
   b. Fall. I don't care if you call me a Basic Bitch, just let me wear my blanket scarf and drink my PSL in peace.
   c. Winter! Nothing's better than the holiday season, sitting by a fireplace, snuggled underneath a blanket.

d. Spring. It's perfect: not too hot, not too cold, and everything flowering is lovely.

2. What's your ideal level of humidity?
   a. So humid I want to feel like I'm walking through a steam bath.
   b. I want the air to be crisp and clear, thanks! Let me pretend I'm on a mountainside.
   c. It needs to be so dry that when I step outside it's like I can *feel* the hydration being leached from my skin.
   d. A little bit of humidity is nice—I don't mind having my hair look a little fluffier and my skin a little dewy.

3. What temperature is your perfect day?
   a. Hot, hot, HOT. Anything below 75 degrees is a disgrace and a waste of my time.
   b. 45 to 60 degrees would be perfect. My body would love me so much: I wouldn't be sweating, nor would I be shivering!
   c. Call me Mr. Freeze, because I want it to be 45 and below only. I want to be so thoroughly covered in layers and blankets that it looks like I'm wearing everything I own.
   d. 60 to 75 degrees. I really *do* only want to need a light jacket when I go outside!

4. What's the highlight of your day?
   a. Hanging out at the beach or by a pool. There's nothing more relaxing than lounging outside.

b. Going to an open-air flea market. It's like treasure hunting, and you can usually find something good to eat there.

c. Cuddling on the couch with my dog, reading. Not leaving the house all day. Incredible.

d. Taking a walk through the park. It's good exercise, it's free, and it's chill.

5. Say you *have* to spend time with people on this day. What do you do?

a. See an outdoor movie. Make it a picnic, potluck, and BYOB. You can talk (quietly) if you want, and if the movie sucks, you can leave!

b. Hang out at a coffee shop with a close friend. Catch up, or just read together. Maybe work on that screenplay you always think about?

c. Have a board game night with friends. You can just hang out in leggings and a sweatshirt with lots of snacks. Just beware of anyone who's super competitive.

d. Go watch a baseball game. Even if sports aren't your thing, you can grab two cheap seats (minor league games are especially inexpensive) and drink beer and eat hot dogs in the sunshine with your friends.

RESULTS: IF YOU PICKED ...

Mostly A's: Try hand-lettering (aka calligraphy). All you need is the proper pen and paper to practice—it's easy to take with you if you're traveling, or if you're hanging out at home on your couch. If you like to journal, this will only up your game, and at the very least, your mom will absolutely love to see her name fancily written on her birthday card envelopes.

Mostly B's: Study up on tarot cards. Perfect if you're witchily inclined, but even if you're not, this frequently misunderstood but now super-trendy hobby is both fun and vaguely therapeutic! Tarot card reading also involves a lot of storytelling, so if you're creatively inclined, this will be a great activity. It will also make you incredibly popular among your friends, who will all want readings themselves.

Mostly C's: Take up baking. Make no mistake—baking is not for the faint of heart. If you've ever watched *The Great British Bake Off* (remember in season five when Paul Hollywood actually uttered, in all seriousness, "You have to understand the philosophy of how a rough puff pastry works"??) or an equivalent, you know this to be true. Baking is difficult but also incredibly rewarding! Not to mention, obviously, tasty.

Mostly D's: Take up bird-watching! You think I'm joking, but before you fly the coop (ha!), hear me out. Bird-watching is perfect in the springtime weather that you love: all of our feathered friends are coming back after a long winter away to nest, and it's a pleasant, relaxing outdoor activity that you can make as easy (a stroll through your local park) or as difficult (an actual hike in the mountains) as you like. Just, uh, remember to bring a hat in case of any unexpected "presents" from above.

PROS AND CONS OF MOVING BACK TO YOUR HOMETOWN

This one goes out to all of you folks who live far from your hometown, and whose parents are constantly—either explicitly or implicitly—asking you to move back home already. Part of you is like, "Hell, no, not in a million years," because sometimes it seems like the love you feel for your parents is directly correlated to the number of miles you have between you, but another part of you is tempted at times to move back home where everything seems simpler and easier, not to mention cheaper (unless your hometown is New York City or San Francisco, in which case, you're out of luck).

If you had a partner or kids, moving home might be complicated, but since it's just you, it could be really easy. Of course, there *is* your job, and your friends, and the life you've made in your adopted city, but putting aside all of that for a minute, consider the following:

PROS:
- Increased chances of homemade cooking. Listen: you're a grown-ass adult and when you moved out, it was no longer your parents' responsibility to cook all your meals for you. *But* if one is offered to you on a regular basis, well, who are you to turn it down! As

we all know, anything someone makes for you always tastes better than if you made it yourself.

- Handyman help. Landlords and building managers are unreliable, and if you're lucky enough to afford your own place (congrats: looks like *someone* was able to lay off the avocado toast for a while), you definitely may need help when something breaks or if looking it up on YouTube and wikiHow just isn't working out. Whether it's your dad, your mom, your sibling, or your great-uncle who's the handy person in your family, it's nice to have reliable help around.

- All jokes aside, it *can* be nice to have a family support system nearby. Sometimes it's good when you have a bad day just to go to your childhood home and be with people who have seen you at your absolute worst and yet are required to/still love you, anyway!

CONS:

- Expect your parents to become a lot more vocal and involved in your love life. If you catch your dad asking you how OkCupid works, make sure you check your phone later just to make sure he hasn't meddled in your account—and maybe change your password to something that's *not* your birthday while you're at it.

- Impromptu drop-ins may become a Thing. You gave your parents the spare key in case of *emergencies*, but they seem to use that word *liberally*, and thank God your romantic life is in the toilet, anyway, because bringing someone home only to inadvertently meet the parents on the first date would be the absolute worst.

- Familial obligations will intensify. Obviously, when you lived on the other side of the country you weren't obligated to go to Aunt Carol's "twenty-ninth" birthday party or your second cousin's vow renewal, but now that you're home, if it's not a family obligation every couple of weekends, it's the expectation that you will be home for every Sunday family dinner, no ifs, ands, or buts about it.

WHAT EVERY SINGLE PERSON NEEDS TO HAVE

Life is tough* for a single person. Cooking for one is the pits (cooking in big batches is more economical, but how boring is it to eat layered salads in mason jars for days on end?), there are so many Groupon vacation specials meant for two people (if life were a rom-com, this would be a perfect setup premise, but alas, it's not), and don't even get me started on carnival and amusement park rides (is there anything sadder than riding a Ferris wheel by yourself?).

Being single in a world so focused on coupling is like being a left-handed person in a right-handed person's world: mildly irritating at best, infuriating at worst. Luckily, there are some ways you can make your life as a single person better, and most of them involve stuff. In the words of *Parks and Recreation*'s Tom Haverford, "Love fades away. But things . . . things are forever." Sounds like totally normal, emotionally well-adjusted advice to me!

Below are some basics that every single person should

---

* It is not that tough.

have in this day and age to make it through (you probably already have some of them, TBH):

- **Roku Subscription:** If you don't have a smart TV that can bundle all of your various subscriptions for you, then you absolutely need a Roku. It's a must. That way you can easily flip between *The Crown* on Netflix, *Bob's Burgers* reruns on Hulu, *Why Women Kill* on CBS All Access, *The Mandalorian* on Disney Plus, and *Fleabag* rewatches on Amazon Prime. I mean, come on, how else will you fill your idle time if you don't have a significant other? A *book*? Grow up.

- **AirPods/Headphones:** These can't just be *any* old headphones. We're going for subtlety here; the subtler, the better. If you can hide it in your hair (especially if you have short hair), then that's the goal. Besides being great for helping you to tune out all of the noise while walking down the street (including catcalls, ugh), it's great for tuning out nosy relatives and family friends during parties as they ask their usual questions. After all, what Aunt Carol doesn't know can't hurt her, right?

- **Keurig Coffee Maker:** What's the point of having a regular coffee maker if there's just one of you, right? And before you say that it's for "entertaining," please be realistic and honest with yourself here. You're among friends, not humble-bragging/lying on HGTV. How often do you *actually* entertain, especially the type of entertaining in which coffee is required? You're going to be pouring a glass of Trader Joe's cabernet sauvignon at your parties, not coffee. (But try to get the reusable

Keurig cups that you can just pack ground coffee beans into—we're trying to save the environment here!)

- **Weighted Blanket:** Originally I was going to say something like "body pillow," but that just seemed a little too on-the-nose and sad, like that blowup doll Aunt Carol gave you for Christmas as a joke without realizing it was actually an inflatable sex doll. Besides, everyone knows that weighted blankets are the new body pillows. Not only are they excellent at keeping you warm during long, harsh winters, they can also soothe symptoms of anxiety and make you feel more stable and at ease.

- **Matching Pajama Set:** You're probably, like, matching pajama set? For *whom*? Aren't my ex's oversized shirt that I never gave back and my ratty plaid pajama pants from high school good enough? First of all, while those clothes are perfectly fine, I guess, I promise, one, you can find a pajama set that's just as comfortable, and two, you're getting a matching pajama set for *yourself*. When you're lounging about your apartment for the entire day, you'll feel a lot more like you're indulging in self-care and less like you're guilty for seemingly doing nothing, instead of your chores, bills, etc. Pajama sets don't need to be uncomfortable, expensive, or even particularly sexy—they just need to match. (10/10 would also recommend a matching robe and some slippers to complete the look.)

- **A Hobby:** Listen, some people already think that singles are just sad, pathetic individuals who sit around doing nothing, bemoaning being single and wishing they weren't. We all know that's emphatically not true, but we shouldn't give anyone reason to believe otherwise. If you already have hobbies, great! If you don't, feel free to consult the quiz *Create Your Perfect Date and We'll Give You a Millennial-Approved Solitary Hobby to Take Up* on page 11. Solitary activities are always good (especially for the introverted type), but social activities are also great. You can sign up for classes and activities at local community centers, and of course, there are always ways to find real-life meetups of like-minded people through the internet.

- **A Vibrator and an Imagination:** This seems pretty self-explanatory, and honestly, very much expected. As we all know, just because you're in a relationship doesn't mean you're guaranteed orgasms (*cue laughter that becomes increasingly strangled*)! But luckily, that's the entire job of a vibrator and, depending on what kind you get, it will get the job done in exactly the way you want. Just don't forget to use lube, and clean your toys regularly, okay? You kids have fun now!

II.

Excuses, Excuses

You shouldn't have to justify your single status to anyone, for any reason, but it seems like no one else has gotten the hint yet. Sometimes you can succinctly articulate a reason, sometimes you can charmingly and easily brush off the invasive queries, and sometimes you don't have the energy or patience to entertain the offensive-yet-somehow-socially acceptable questions regarding your single and/or childless state. Well, from the serious to the silly, we've got you covered next time you're asked (which, alas, is all too often), and telling the other person to F*** off isn't an option.

REASONS WHY YOU JUST DON'T WANT TO BE SET UP RIGHT NOW, THANKS, AUNT CAROL: A MAD LIBS/FILL-IN-THE-BLANK ACTIVITY

Hi, Aunt Carol! Yes, I *did* get your email with _____'s *(name)* phone number, their latest album of Facebook photos, and all of the facts you remembered about them at 5:32 a.m. when you wrote me that email. Yep, a retired person's day does start early! It is *so kind* of you to think of me and I'm sure that _____ *(name)* is very *nice*, but I'm just not interested in dating. Why? Well, I'm super busy at work, what with the _____ *(activity)*, especially since my boss _____ *(verb)* the _____ *(noun)*. That corporate rat race; it's killer!

Also, my personal life is an absolute *mess*. Last week, my apartment became infested with _____ *(noun)* and it's driving me and my cat crazy. My cat _____ *(name)* is so agitated that she _____ *(verb)* the _____ *(noun)*. And my landlord is no help! He told me to _____ *(verb)* the _____ *(noun)*. I have to take care of my home before I can even *think* about inviting someone into it!

And remember my upcoming trip to _____ *(location)*? I have to plan for that. I'm going to go see _____ *(location)* and of course I'm going to _____ *(verb)* the _____ *(noun)*. It's a must-do, according to all of the guides.

Aunt Carol, you're right. It's like you're always telling me: I'll never get a partner if I don't _____ (verb) and _____ (verb), and if I don't start taking dating seriously, I'll end up _____ (adjective) and _____ (adjective). But I think it's best if I stay single! And also, to be honest, _____ (name) doesn't really seem like my type. I tend to prefer them _____ (adjective) and _____ (adjective).

I know you're trying to look out for me, and I always appreciate it, Aunt Carol. You and _____ (name) have been married for _____ (length of time) and you're very happy together. Well, except for that time _____ (name) ran off with the _____ (noun). But we don't need to get into that. Anyway, I need to go make the rounds with the other aunts, but it was great catching up, and wonderful to see you, as always!

WHY MILLENNIALS AREN'T HAVING KIDS

Now that we're in our late twenties and early thirties, a pretty big concern for adults in our lives when they find out that we're single is: *But what about children? Don't you want to have b a b i e s? Those eggs (or sperm) don't stay fresh forever, you know!* Besides the general mortification of having near-complete strangers discuss the "freshness" of your body like you're about to head to the meat market, the idea of having children in this day and age is so unfathomable to me that sometimes you just have to laugh (or scream!). The circumstances in which our parents had kids are vastly different from what we millennials have been given. Factors that make having kids incredibly difficult, bordering on unrealistic, for our generation, include, but are not limited to:

- **The Economy**: A baby? In *this* economy? Do you know what most people consider their babies? Their college degrees: 42 percent of people ages eighteen to twenty-nine have student loan debt, thus many of us consider our subsequent degrees our "children," given the percentage of our paycheck going toward paying it off. And boomers want us to consider adding *real* children to that? At least a bachelor's degree just sits there quietly in a corner of the bedroom and doesn't poop its pants constantly! And it *may* lead to getting a job with decent pay *and* benefits *and* maybe a few sick days and a vacation. Can a grandchild do that, Mom, hmm?

- **Global Warming**: A recent headline said that the Earth might burn itself out by 2050, and while at times the idea of shuffling off this mortal coil sounds appealing (especially on a Monday morning), that's only thirty years from now, very much still in our lifetime. In 2050 a good chunk of us won't even qualify for social security yet, if social security is even still a thing by the time we're eligible (ha! Good one). And people want our generation to bring *babies* into this world so they can witness the fall of the planet during the prime of their lives?? *Is* there SPF thick enough for a baby's fragile skin to withstand nuclear summer? You know how, when you were younger, your parents got you a goldfish and told you that if you took care of the goldfish then maybe you could get a dog? Well, the Earth is our goldfish, Mother, so maybe if you don't kill it you can get a grandkid.

- **Parents Gonna Parent:** Sometimes it's incredible to think about the fact that our parents want *us* to have children when in many ways they still treat us like *we* are children! And yes, to them we will *Mariah Carey voice* always be their babies, but your dad still doesn't think you can do your taxes on your own and your mom, like clockwork, no matter how much you protest, continues to schedule your twice-yearly dentist appointments without asking you. They mean well, and yeah, it's nice not to have to worry about those things, but if they don't think you can take care of yourself, why are they so insistent that you're ready to take care of an *actual* child??

REASONS TO TELL YOUR MOM'S COLLEGE BEST FRIEND WHO'S INTO CRYSTALS WHY YOU'RE SINGLE BASED ON YOUR ZODIAC SIGN

You're not even that into astrology, really. (Not like your co-worker or your roommate, who's constantly refreshing the Co-Star app.) And when your mom's best friend from college (formerly known as Helen, currently going by Starfire Moonbeam) is asking you about your moon sign, your rising sign, and which sign rules your Venus, it's like she's speaking another language.

As tempting as it is to give in and tell her to back off (privacy is a foreign concept to her now that she lives on the outskirts of town in a co-op you're pretty sure is actually a cult), you know she means well when she solemnly tells you that the thought of you "moving through the universe as a single soul" keeps her up at night, and that "if your essence doesn't merge with another's, you are not fully engaging with the world as the Goddess Mother intended." Telling her that you're too busy or focused on your career or just aren't that into dating and romance won't fly here, so maybe it's time to try speaking her language. It can't hurt, right? Look up your sun sign (but nothing else, don't worry) and read the corresponding horoscope below to hopefully get Starfire off your back.

Aries: Other people tend to find your high energy abrasive and are intimidated by your sunny confidence. You have yet to find the complementary spirit that seeks to brighten your flame, not dampen it.

Taurus: You're a homebody who prefers the simple pleasures in life. Many people these days are concerned with fleeting, flashy things, and though at times you long for a like-minded individual to welcome into your home, you're content to nest alone for now.

Gemini: Your life was once joined with another of Earth's inhabitants, but you recently parted ways. (And no matter what you hear from anyone, it wasn't your fault!) They frequently misinterpreted your open-minded, dynamic ways.

27

Cancer: It's just that you're in an emotionally fragile place right now and feel that inviting another soul into your life's journey would only muddle your path at this time.

Leo: You have big plans for yourself, and your ambition is not to be thwarted. You simply cannot focus your spotlight on anything or anyone else.

Virgo: Currently, you are meticulously and thoroughly searching for a mate with all of the attention to detail befitting your sign, and will of course give updates if there are promising candidates.

Libra: The life you have curated is, at this time, perfectly balanced. To disturb such harmony would be an insult to the Goddess; at a more opportune time you'll begin to invite romantic elements into your life again.

Scorpio: Despite existing in a time in which many your age have a fear of labels, you would enjoy being in a committed, loyal relationship. Alas, such partners are scarce, so instead you're focusing on cultivating equally satisfying sexual relationships. (Are you blushing, Starfire?)

Sagittarius: You're evaluating your options to see which of them, if any, are compatible enough to be your fellow traveler on life's voyage. It is entirely likely that none of them will be able to hold your interest for long, each potential suitor a fleeting pit stop.

Capricorn: There is a plan in place to find and attract a partner, but you also have many methodical processes in progress for various aspects of your life, so it may take some time for your dating goals to come to fruition.

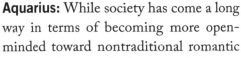

Aquarius: While society has come a long way in terms of becoming more open-minded toward nontraditional romantic and sexual relationships, unfortunately the type of relationship you desire is not widely practiced. Surely, Starfire, you of all people understand the narrow-minded restrictions under which we live!

Pisces: You've recently separated your essence from another's and, while this dissolution of intermingling souls was saddening, it was also necessary, and you're currently taking time to sift through the myriad emotions you feel in its wake before you begin your search anew.

III.

Deep Breaths: Coping Mechanisms for the Single Person

Sometimes, an excuse and a smile aren't enough to get out of certain situations: sometimes, you have to just grit your teeth, turn that grimace into a grin, and bear it. Being a reasonable adult is the worst: remember the days in which you could just throw a tantrum with very few repercussions? If only we could go back to our toddler years. But, we can't, so instead we have to trick our brains into thinking we're less miserable than we are, and while that's not a good long-term solution, for one night, it's good enough.

DISSOCIATIVE DAYDREAMS/
MINDFULNESS ACTIVITIES

So you're riding solo at *(circle one)* your best friend's baby shower/your sister's wedding rehearsal dinner/your cousin's graduation party/a required work holiday party, and you somehow end up talking to the most self-involved, boring person there, who sees you as a vaguely sentient, empty vessel for them to project all of their hopes and dreams upon. You've been mistaken for someone who actually cares about the minute details of their *(circle one)* recent dental surgery/D&D campaign/Florida resort vacation/house renovation. Escape is impossible, and you've resignedly pasted on your best, fake "active listening" face, just like your mother taught you. But that doesn't mean all is lost! Retreat into the fortress that is your beautiful, weird mind and get lost in intricate fantasies and irreverent "what if" scenarios. For example:

- Lovingly plot out your dream date (platonic or romantic) with your celebrity of choice. Whether it's going to a dog park with Chris Evans (he laughs at all of the dogs' antics in his typical hand-on-chest, head-thrown-back pose, *don't you dare pretend like you don't know what I'm talking about*), having brunch with John Cho (yes, he is genuinely interested in hearing about the minutiae of your work drama with Brenda from HR, and would you like a bite of his avocado toast? He's happy to share.), attending a music festival with Tessa Thompson (she always remembers to tell you to hydrate or reapply sunscreen, and knows exactly which bands to see and which ones to skip), or even just hanging out at home while Oscar Isaac makes you a delicious cocktail (he might even throw in a back rub—who are we kidding, *of course* he'll throw in a back rub), this is the time to indulge!

- My roommate and I like to play this little game where we ask each other, "What should I reward myself with for getting through this awful [mildly uncomfortable] situation?" Because, as you know, we millennials grew up in a culture of instant gratification and participation trophies, according to baby boomers. (Which generation created and then raised millennials in such a culture, hmmmm?? Toddlers can't mass-produce their own participation trophies, Geoff!!! But I digress . . .) In actuality, it's because capitalism is a drug, and when big things like the economy and climate change majorly suck (see: *Why Millennials Aren't Having Kids* on page 24), then taking solace in the goodness of small joys is all we have left. Contemplate what will soothe you after being asked three times in a row if you're still sad about how Things Ended with Kevin (honestly, Kevin was a blip, you always forget you dated him, and you are not sad about how things slowly and passionlessly dissolved). These little treats can range from doing a face mask at home while diving into that TV show/fanfic/pint of ice cream that you've been saving for a tough day like today, to stopping at your favorite fast-food place and ordering that perfect combo of French fries and milkshake, to going into your favorite store and buying a pretty bauble that you don't *need* but would never buy otherwise. Give yourself something to look forward to! Otherwise, this event will stretch on like a dark tunnel of nothingness, and it's best to save that sort of existential dread for 3 a.m. insomnia or Deep Shower Thoughts!

- Is there a movie you've seen so many times you can quote it almost entirely by memory? One in which you know every scene, every wardrobe change, every minute look and tone? Go ahead and play that movie in your head, start to finish. Unlike this snooze fest of a party, it'll be a guaranteed good time. Finally, knowing that Mr. Darcy dives into that pond at exactly the four-hour, twenty-three-minute mark will actually come in handy! If you want to get incredibly creative, you can even imagine people from the party in the movie: my personal favorite is picturing a work nemesis as Regina George from *Mean Girls*, especially during that iconic bus scene.

- What will the new animal trend be? We've cycled through owls and foxes and llamas and flamingos, but what's next? Pandas? Dolphins? Honestly, we can do better. We're playing it safe as a society! We could go quirkier, we could get weirder (owls are pretty weird, though—have you ever seen one turn its freaky little head around?). Think about *this*: raccoons. They're perfect! They're cute enough to make into wide-eyed cartoons for toddler T-shirts but not *so* cute that the average millennial wouldn't want to buy a mug with the handle as a striped tail. Whether we want to admit it or not, we can all relate a bit to a vicious little night-dweller who stays out too late consuming trash, and I'm ready to see the raccoon get the recognition she deserves!!

- What would a modern episode of a beloved, now syndicated TV show be about? For the purpose of this exercise, let's pick *30 Rock*. Which US senator/representative, in a desperate attempt to be cool and pander to a younger demographic, would appear on the show? Perhaps as a subplot, both Jenna and Tracy are in a feud with James Corden, who they claim stole the idea for Carpool Karaoke from them. Liz Lemon, fed up with the coolness/weirdness of people on Tinder and Bumble, might accidentally create a dating app called Frumple. *Frumple*, for people who just want to stay at home and work on their night cheese. You wish you were at home on your couch with some night cheese right now. Oh, God, you can't think about night cheese too hard, otherwise that longing will show up on your politely blank face.

- If you won the $100 million Powerball, what would you do with the money? Better yet, you have to pick one practical, one philanthropic, one fun, and one ridiculous rich-person thing to divide your money among (so you can't just say you'd save it all, although who actually would ever do that??).

VENUS IS NOWHERE TO BE FOUND,
AKA THE SINGLE PERSON TAROT SPREAD

For those of you who aren't into tarot or astrology or any witchy stuff (yet), feel free to skip this section. For those of you who *are*, welcome. I don't know about you, but I like to do a tarot spread at least once a week; it helps clear my mind while simultaneously focusing on thoughts and emotions that I normally push aside in a desperate attempt to function, hahaha, ohmygod. In a way, tarot cards and readings can be therapeutic (although by no means do they replace actual therapy!).

The following spread can be done whenever you want, but was specifically made for giving you clarity and strength when having to go to or endure something (or someone) that you don't want to, aka, when you're forced to mingle. Staying home in your safe and cozy apartment is not always an option, alas, so the cards are here to help!

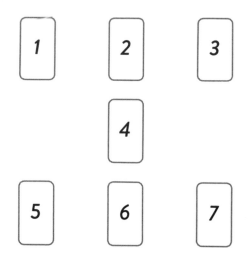

1. What are my intentions going into this encounter?
2. What will give me strength in this situation?
3. What will hinder me from succeeding?
4. What do I need to release?
5. What am I able to control in this situation?
6. What am I not able to control?
7. What lessons can I learn here?

HOW TO SURVIVE SEEING YOUR EX: HOT TIPS

Did you shudder just reading this title? If so, I don't blame you. I don't know about you, but the idea of running into any of my exes, even the ones with whom the breakups were amicable, makes me want to crawl into a hole and never come out. Here's to being a hermit forever!

Sometimes, however, the universe doles out cruel and unusual punishments (or life is just uncontrollable chaos that we can never predict, whichever) and you happen to run into them—on the street, at the grocery store, leaving the gym, wherever. The odds increase when you're both back home for the holidays, ugh. It's even worse if they're with friends, family, or, heaven forbid, their new SO. *Why*, you ask God, whether or not you believe in Him, *are you putting me through this?* While I can't answer that question, I can, at the very least, give you tips on how to get through it, the absolute worst situation in which you are "forced to mingle":

- I'm sure, in any dream (or nightmare?) scenario in which you run into your ex, you look your absolute best, like, favorite outfit, freshly cut hair, just so sleek and polished that they forget that the majority of the time you were together you were in your favorite raggedy college sweatpants. If you happen to run into them while looking that glamorous, I congratulate you. If, however, your hair is sweaty and matted from your recent Pilates class, and you're in workout gear that should've been replaced two presidents ago, my best advice is to fake it until you make it. Lift your chin up high and resolutely ignore that bead of sweat that's dripping down your temple. À la Queen Elizabeth II, never complain, never explain. And *never* apologize for your appearance in front of said ex, and instead maintain a cheerful (self-deprecating if you must, but try to avoid that) attitude until the nightmare has passed and you can go home and take a long shower to scrub away any and all feelings you have about this encounter.

- Unless your breakup was absolutely horrific, unfortunately you cannot run away from them and simply must endure this interaction. As painful as it may be, you have to be polite. Similar to the old refrain about pretending your audience is in their underwear while public speaking, pretend that your ex, well, isn't your ex. The closest thing you should strive for is to pretend that they're a business acquaintance and treat them like one: being cool, cordial, and slightly overly formal is the way to go. To me, being formal translates to being impersonal, while still being polite and maintaining the upper hand.

- Here's the thing: no matter what they ask you, *don't lie*. I don't care if your life is in utter shambles: making up bold-faced lies, like you've been promoted to your company's CEO and are dating Chris Evans and have a brand-new, fabulous apartment, is tempting, but can easily be proven wrong with two clicks of a Google search. I also don't care if your ex looks better than they ever have, with their arm wrapped around an equally gorgeous new partner. I sympathize, but I don't care, because lying will just give you more anxiety! If you must, just put a "positive spin" on the truth. For instance, if your job sucks, find some kernel of truth about one thing you like about it, and emphasize that. Like, say your current job is fine, but not as fulfilling as you want it to be, and you are looking at other options. If you're unemployed, sidestep any questions about your old job, and discuss the new jobs and fields you're currently applying to, etc.

- Okay, but what if your ex *is* with someone new and you aren't? Isn't it okay to lie then? No, it's not! If you absolutely must, you can say that you're dating around right now and not looking for anything serious, *wink wink*, or you can say that you just don't have time in your life for romance, if it bothers you that much. But there's no shame in being single, no matter how much anyone says otherwise, including your ex.

- Keep things short and concise; get in and get out. Being impersonal also means that you don't need to feel obligated to stand there while they ramble about their life. Make it clear (if it's not already to them) that you're both adults, but you're not friends, and neither of you needs to act like you are. Exchange very surface-level pleasantries, tell them to have a nice night (or nice life, if you're feeling just a smidgen petty), and hightail it out of there (a brisk, purposeful walk with perfect posture is best here).

IV.

Just a Sweet, Sweet (Single-Person) Fantasy

Single or not, doesn't everyone constantly walk around with a running narrative in their head of perfect/ridiculous things that would never happen in real life? It's just that the fantasies of single people who just want to be left alone might have a different flavor than other people's. There's no shame in that game! If it helps you get through the day, there's no harm in that. Indulge to your heart's content!

PUT TOGETHER YOUR IDEAL BENEFITS PACKAGE AND WE'LL GIVE YOU A FAKE SIGNIFICANT OTHER TO DISCUSS AT YOUR NEXT EVENT

People keep asking us single folks what we're looking for in a significant other, and sure, that's important to think about if you're actually looking for that kind of thing, *but* do you know what people rarely ask us about that we're *always* looking for? Health care! That beautiful, intangible "adult" thing that we never worried about until we were twenty-six and unceremoniously kicked off our parents' plans. Now we're left to click back and forth between healthcare.gov and our company's website, seeing if our accident-prone selves can survive in this world with a high deductible and whether our co-pay is low enough that we can afford the therapy we so desperately need. That's what's really important here, Aunt Carol, not setting me up with your neighbor's godchild!

Listen. In an ideal world, we would all get the benefits package *and* the partner of our dreams. But in this version of the universe, sometimes we get none or part of those things (medical with limited dental and an occasional hookup who "doesn't like to put labels on things"). Also in an ideal world? People would accept that someone is single without batting an eye or asking uncomfortable follow-up questions or offering to set them up. If we lived in *that* world, perhaps we wouldn't *need* to stoop to making someone up just to get some peace and quiet at the next cul-de-sac cookout. But, folks, here we are!

This quiz will indulge in that beautiful fantasy world of naturopathic medicine coverage and tolerance combined with the groundwork for creating the "perfect" partner . . . for tonight, anyway:

1. How many doctor's visits per year should your insurance cover?
   a. 0. Doctors are needle-happy quacks, and the herbs in my garden will heal any ailment just fine, thanks.
   b. 1–2. I would like a professional to do the usual: tell me to lose ten pounds and say my blood pressure is too high but proclaim that I'm "basically" healthy and should live another year. Joy.
   c. 3+. The most meaningful relationship I have is with WebMD and I'm convinced that every particle of dust is out to get me. I need someone to tell me I'm not dying at least once a month!!

2. Pick one only: dental coverage or vision coverage.
   a. Neither. Teeth are bones, and as long as they don't break, then why do you need to have them cleaned? You don't have the bones on the *inside* of your body cleaned! As for your eyes, glasses companies are capitalistic enterprises that prey on people's fear of their entropic bodies. If you can't see perfectly, who cares! You can get by with a blurry outline of Aunt Carol.
   b. Vision. Worse comes to worst, there are dental implants, but you can't replace your eyes!

c. Dental. If the idea of having a mouthful of *rotting bones* doesn't freak you out, what will?

3. Would you rather have a lower deductible or a lower out-of-pocket maximum?
   a. I understand all of those words separately, but they lose all meaning one after the other.
   b. A lower deductible. I usually stay pretty healthy throughout the year and just go to regular check-ups, dental cleanings, and perhaps the occasional physical therapy session.
   c. A lower out-of-pocket maximum. I tore my ACL twice in the past four years—I'm a goddamn disaster of a human being.

4. Pick one reproductive-focused service to be covered: birth control, freezing your eggs, or adoption fund.
   a. Freezing my eggs. The way the dating landscape looks now, there's no way in hell I'm going to find someone to date/marry/have kids with before my ovaries shrivel up completely.
   b. Birth control. I don't even want to *think* about having kids in the next few years, thanks.
   c. Adoption fund. I don't see any point in bringing more children into this dumpster fire of a world, but I certainly wouldn't mind giving a good home to a child already in it.

5. Select one self-care add-on: therapist, nutritionist, or gym membership.

a. Nutritionist. My body is a temple, and considering the amount of toxins and gross chemicals in food these days, it's best if I know exactly what I should and can consume.

b. Therapist. Who wouldn't benefit from talking things out with a licensed professional who is trained to help navigate the rocky waters that we call life?

c. Gym membership. My life can be so stressful and rigid, and the best way for me to relieve that stress sometimes is releasing it through physical activity.

6. Lastly, would you want any unnecessary, completely cosmetic/beauty procedures to be covered?

a. Nope. No thanks, I don't want any injections or sculpting or augments or decreases or whatever. Society and its gross beauty standards can kiss my ass.

b. I don't want anything major, but honestly, it *would* be nice to have a facial or a massage covered, especially after an unusually horrendous event. Aunt Carol's negativity is aging.

c. Yes, as many as possible. Give me enough Botox to look as numb on the outside as I feel on the inside!

RESULTS: IF YOU PICKED . . .

Mostly A's: You and Devin met in a yoga class, and you, while trying to regulate your breathing in downward dog, couldn't help but be impressed with their perfect pigeon pose. Devin loves to make kombucha, spend afternoons weeding in their community garden, and explain to you what the different recycling numbers mean (they made you a chart; it hangs on your fridge). You've been dating for two months, and your future breakup will occur when Devin decides to be That White Person and grows dreads, no matter how many articles on cultural appropriation you send their way. Yikes!

Mostly B's: You and Chris met at a hockey game your friends dragged you to; you couldn't care less about the sport, but they had an extra ticket, and you take great amusement in befuddling the Serious Sports Fans around you by shouting to the players as though they're Magic Mike strippers instead of professional athletes. Chris was sitting next to you and, to their credit, was also mostly amused by your outlandish behavior. Chris enjoys playing in a rec-league softball team, microbreweries, and going to the farmers' market on Sundays. You've been dating for five months, and when pressed, you'll say that your amicable split will happen when you both decide that you don't really have that much physical chemistry and are better off as friends. Alas.

Mostly C's: You met Alex in a bar, but it's not what you think: both of your workplaces happened to have happy-hour events in each half of the bar, and you ran into each other (literally) on the way back from the bathrooms. Alex looked *very* good in that chic blazer, and their ambition was a major turn-on; you spent the rest of the night chatting. Alex enjoys running marathons, doing crossword puzzles in pen, and doesn't believe in sleeping in. Ever. You've been dating for nearly four months, and sadly, while Alex's ambition is what drew you to them, ultimately their commitment to their job overshadows any commitment to you. You break up just before the next big event. Tragic!

WISH-FULFILLMENT MOVIES THAT NETFLIX SHOULD TOTALLY MAKE

Netflix has really stepped up its game when it comes to their original movies. They range from sweet book adaptations like *To All the Boys I've Loved Before* to delightfully ridiculous holiday rom-coms like *The Knight Before Christmas*. Whether viewers are looking for wish fulfillment or just pure bonkers-level escapism, there's a scrap of daydream-level fantasy inherent in each movie.

Those fantasies are not unlike the ones described on page 87, in which elaborate scenarios with *Gilmore Girl*–esque dialogues are constructed and could include a chance meeting with your celebrity crush, the perfect verbal quip against your nemesis, or perhaps closure on something you've never quite moved on from—aka, the key component of many Netflix movies.

Below are some movie ideas that Netflix should absolutely take and make that will absolutely fulfill every fantasy. They can't be any worse than some of the ones they've already created, anyway!

Hermitella

The Main Character is exhausted from relentless professional and personal commitments and their life is in utter shambles because they haven't had time to do what they need to do.

In the midst of their busy life, they manage to do a kind deed for an old woman, who later reveals herself to be a fairy godmother! (Just go with me here.) The Main Character wishes to have absolutely no obligations or commitments for a month and their wish is granted. The rest of the movie is just a montage of them cleaning and organizing their apartment, Marie Kondo style, doing errands they've been putting off for months, grocery shopping, going to the gym, making progress in their enormous To Be Read pile of books by their bedside, and sleeping. Lots of sleeping. They emerge from their hibernation feeling refreshed and rejuvenated!

I'll Be (the Only One) Home for Christmas

Single millennials come back to their hometown for the holidays, dreading well-meaning but invasive questions about their life, particularly why are they single, and when will they give their parents grandchildren. To their complete delight, absolutely no one in their family asks about their dating life unless the millennials themselves bring it up first, and their questions are polite, appropriate follow-ups. The holidays pass enjoyably and without drama, and the millennial is actually looking forward to going home next year!

Sex Outside of the City

The Protagonist, who has a "high-powered" career in The City, comes home to their suburban/rural town for a holiday/funeral/reunion/complex legal matter and reconnects with their childhood best friend of the opposite sex (who is a fully fleshed character with their own hopes, dreams, and obstacles). Despite the wishes of both of their families, they do not fall in love because they're both hella gay, and instead team up to be excellent wing-people for each other with a comedy-of-errors type of narrative. In the end, the Protagonist does not want to, nor do they have to, give up the life they love in The City for their new romantic partner; instead, they agree to take it slow and see what happens, doing long distance! And they remain in contact with their childhood best friend, of course.

12 Days of Closure

The Main Character gets a chance to say exactly what they need to with absolutely zero consequences or repercussions to twelve people in their life, ranging from ex-partners to ex-friends to useless bosses to annoying coworkers to racist relatives. Of course, the Main Character gets to choose the time and place, and obviously they're looking their best when it happens (cool, but not trying too hard). They then are able to say the thing they've always wanted to say, worded in the absolute perfect way that is the correct balance of witty yet sincere, cutting yet not cruel. Everyone reacts in exactly the way the Main Character wants, and if there are any arguments the Main Character always wins them. And the best part? The happy ending is that they finally get to move on.

MILLENNIAL MASH

Remember MASH? You know, that game you played in elementary/middle/let's-be-honest-probably-high-school, too, at sleepovers, on field trips, and at long sports/dance/cheer tournaments? At a time in your life when the future was probably super exciting and something to be fantasized about instead of being super scary and nebulous like a carbon monoxide cloud? Well, who says you can't relive the past, if only for five minutes! Forget about your current worries and go back in time like it's 1999 with this updated version of MASH.

If you've never played before, no worries, because it's actually super simple: Basically this is a Wish Fulfillment game in which, totally by chance, you "determine" your future life. You're able to put in your top choices/dreams, while someone else (usually your friend) will choose some awful options "just for fun."

To determine how you'll figure out this mystical future, usually your friend would draw a "magic swirl," and when you tell them to stop they count the rings. With that number, you "count" your future. For example, if the number of rings is seven, then you count every option in your list, regardless of category, and every seventh option is crossed out. Once you're down to the last option in each category, that's what your future will be. (If you're playing alone, which you probably are—no offense—just pick a random number between one and ten or roll a pair of dice.) I have to admit, for me, MASH could be nerve-racking back in the day, even though I knew it wasn't real; on the flip side, there were definitely certain MASH sheets of paper that I admit I kept for years after as though it really was an oracle of my future.

Push comes to shove, this can make for a great "fake" story to use at get-togethers if you're single. If you're feeling really daring, you can bring it out no matter how ridiculous it sounds and see if anyone calls you out on it. Honestly, if you say it with enough confidence, I'm sure at the very least any hard-of-hearing great-uncles won't know the difference!

McMansion in cookie-cutter LA neighborhood
Apartment in your favorite city
Shack, aka run-down apartment in Brooklyn with
    five roommates
House in a suburb somewhere

SPOUSE	JOB	# OF KIDS
Favorite celebrity crush	What your mom's job was	0
High school nemesis	Your current job	10
The cute barista	Your dream job	3
Your last ex	The most boring job you can think of	1

VEHICLE	PET	SALARY
Your current vehicle	A cat who tolerates you	Minimum wage
The NYC Subway forever	A dog who loves you	Jeff Bezos money
Your dream car	A parrot who won't shut up	Current wage
Wheelie shoes	No pets, ever	$0

DRAW YOUR "MAGIC SWIRL" HERE:

YOUR MAGIC NUMBER IS: _____

In conclusion: Congratulations, and welcome to your future, courtesy of MASH! In this fantasy, you will be married to _____. You will live in a _____ with your _____ children and your pet, a _____. Your job will be _____, which will pay you _____, and you will commute there in _____.

IF CLASSIC LITERARY HEROINES WERE MODERN-DAY MILLENNIAL WOMEN

If you're familiar with any or all of these women, you know that in their own ways, they're pretty phenomenal, especially for the respective time periods in which they were created. But perhaps, like me, it's bothered you to know that their potential was hampered because of when they were "alive" and their identities as women. Which, so unfair! We all know, for instance, that if Lady Macbeth were alive today, she would be giving Kris Jenner a run for her money.

Following is a further indulgence of some musings on what these ladies would be like if they were both a) real and b) alive today:

Emma Woodhouse: In theory, Emma Woodhouse should be absolutely the most annoying, tone-deaf, spoiled white rich girl alive. In reality, somehow I (and many others) find her simply charming—whether that's because I've been influenced by *Clueless* or Jane Austen is just *that* talented (I'm going to say both), Emma remains an Icon to this day. And you know what? I don't even blame her for getting up in everybody's business, because what *else* was she supposed to do? Work on needlework and calm her dad's neuroses 24/7? No, thanks. Emma is absolutely a woman who needs a career, whether that's managing an entire company or, better yet, being an organizational psychologist, where she can sweep into various companies throughout the country (with her trusty assistant, Harriet Smith, by her side) and tell them exactly how they should be doing things for maximum efficiency and employee happiness. And if that's where she *happens* to meet some uptight-accountant-lawyer type named Mr. Knightley (who's age appropriate and doesn't go around saying gross things like "I've loved you since you were thirteen"), then all the better! Equally likely is that Emma would be a serial monogamist who would be quite happy having multiple semiserious relationships throughout her life but would be entirely too busy to settle down completely.

Jane Eyre: Oh, Jane. Man, do I love Jane Eyre a whole lot, and think that she in particular Deserved Better than the circumstances she was dealt in her eponymous book. Much like Elizabeth Bennet, Jane also didn't settle to marry one of various men just for stability (I'm looking particularly at *you*, creepy cousin St. John Rivers). And to be honest, I was so bummed when she ended up marrying Rochester at the end of the book. Hot take: We just *think* Rochester is dreamy because he was most recently played by Michael Fassbender, but he's actually a terrible person! Listen, the heart wants what it wants, but if Jane had more options in life (regardless of the money she inherited) I don't think she would've actually married him. Jane had an inherently independent spirit and throughout the book was given opportunities to travel, but only with men as their wife (France with Mr. Rochester; India with St. John). Ideally, Jane would be able to see the world on her own terms. Honestly, it would be great to see Jane develop lifelong friendships for emotional support rather than relying on men who only see her as a potential wife.

Jo March: Confession time: As a child after first reading *Little Women*, I was absolutely livid when author Louisa May Alcott a) had Jo not marry Laurie, b) had Laurie marry Amy (sigh, *Amy*), and c) had Jo marry gross old Professor Bhaer. While I'm still pretty cranky about point c), I now see that, with wisdom and experience with #fuckbois, having Jo marry Laurie would've been a terrible idea. At most, Jo and Laurie should've just been high school sweethearts who lost their virginity to each other and then broke up when they left for their respective colleges (he bought his way into some Ivy school as a legacy, and she went to an all-girls school— Mount Holyoke or Smith if she wanted to stick closer to home, or Scripps if she wanted to get as far away as possible). For the sake of the story, let's say Jo went to Scripps because she wanted to eventually end up in Hollywood, writing scripts for television shows. Would Jo ever marry? To constantly and consistently compare Jo to her creator, Louisa May, who herself never married, seems like a cop-out, but at the same time, it seems unlikely that modern-day Jo would ever marry, unless it was to someone who was just as obsessed with their craft/work as Jo is. Or, you know, she'd at least marry someone superhot, like Cate Blanchett.

Anne Shirley: If anyone ever thinks that gingers don't have souls (ahem, *South Park*), then they've never read *Anne of Green Gables*, because the redheaded Anne Shirley has enough soul for about five people combined. She's dreamy and adventurous and finds wonder in everyday things, which this little cynic finds pretty noble. (Wonder and joy? In *this* political climate? In *this* economy? Sounds fake.) But regardless of whether she's living in the late nineteenth century or the early twenty-first, Anne Shirley's indomitable spirit would be a constant. Of all the women on this list, she was the only one who went to college, and she had a short-lived career as a teacher and principal before she married the dreamy and devoted Gilbert Blythe (side question: Would Gilbert qualify as a modern-day "Wife Guy"?). Anne still would've gone to college and married Gilbert, but she wouldn't have been a teacher. She loved writing short stories and poetry and absolutely would've pursued her MFA. Her lifelong goal would be to have a short story published in *The New Yorker*, and in the meantime she'd have a fake Instagram just for her poetry. (Look out, Atticus!)

Juliet Capulet: I have a lot of sympathy for Juliet Capulet. She gets a bad rap, but I think that's because her and Romeo's story frequently gets misrepresented in pop culture as a romance, when it's actually a tragedy. Both she and Romeo are dismissed as horny teenagers (which, to be fair, they are), but in reality they're pawns in a complex social structure involving their noble, feuding families. Juliet deserved to be a normal teenager. Instead of dying in a crypt as a victim of an interfering weird priest's machinations, modern-day teen-aged Juliet would've totally dated dreamy, sensitive Romeo after meeting at their rival high schools' football game or probably the after party at someone's house. Dating a boy from a "rival" school would've been incredibly mysterious and fun, especially if it got her out of boring business dinners with her dad and his creepy associate Paris (let's be real: this Paris would *not* have been a young Paul Rudd). Alas, all good things must come to an end, including love, because she probably would've dumped Romeo two weeks later for his much hotter, much more interesting friend Mercutio, who, unlike Romeo, emphatically did *not* make and recite terrible, cheesy poetry to her. As for Romeo? He would've been just fine, because that's a guy who bounces back quickly (remember how he claimed he was in love with fair Rosaline until he saw Juliet?). I would say "all's well that ends well," but that's an entirely different story, and, to paraphrase John Mulaney, we don't have time to unpack all of *that*.

Beatrice: The protagonist from the comedy *Much Ado About Nothing* is an MVP and she's truly the greatest. For example: When her enemies-to-lovers boyfriend, Benedick, told her he loved her, she was like, "Okay, you do? Prove it. Go kill your best friend, who broke my cousin's heart and caused her untimely death." She was metal as hell and did what she had to do. An Icon! She's honestly perfect. Could you imagine who she would be in the twenty-first century? The idea is almost too powerful. She would 100 percent have an awesome podcast, at the very least, talking about feminism in some new and nuanced way, with a lot of guest hosts to properly discuss intersectionality. When not podcasting, she would probably spend a lot of her time stumping for progressive female political candidates. (Does she already have a custom-made *Ocasio-Cortez 2028* sticker? Without a doubt.) If Beatrice were American, Thanksgiving would be an absolute nightmare for her family, as she would consider the dinner table just another political battlefield, but you know she would have a great time speaking her mind, as per usual. Would she still marry Benedick? Who can say, but those two would *absolutely* have a lot of "hate" sex before realizing that, oh, wait, they might've caught feelings along the way.

Hester Prynne: Hester of *The Scarlet Letter* was another lady who deserved far, far better than the circumstances in which she lived. Was Puritanical America fun for *anyone?* (The white men and the ministers, probably.) Subjected to wearing that *A* while her lover could hide in plain sight, Hester and her daughter, Pearl, were outcasts for years until finally the truth came out and her late husband's money could ensure that she and Pearl had a life outside of their heinous town. That's cold consolation, though, for the abuses and injustices that Hester was subjected to, so it's far more pleasant to imagine her in modern-day times, in which she could've had more choices as to whether or not to keep Pearl, and if she did, she wouldn't be a moral outcast because of it. Hester was an awesome seamstress, and could've pursued a fashion career (for example, Hester could have become the next Rachel Green à la *Friends*, except obviously unlike Rachel, she wouldn't have gotten back together with Ross, ew), earning a living for her and her child. Dimmesdale and Chillingworth could've lived their lives as deadbeats or whatever, who honestly cares, but Hester would've been just fine (and, to the disgruntlement of her hometown's nosy residents, completely off the grid regarding social media, so they couldn't even cyber-stalk her to see what she was up to).

V.

If You Must Mingle . . .

So you want to get Out There. Intentionally. Dip your toes in the waters of sociability, so to speak. Don't worry, we all have that impulse, no matter how short-lived it might end up being. If you're feeling nervous, that's okay! It's not so bad out there, and if you hate it, you can always retreat. In the meantime, here are ways to make sure that your times among the masses are as good as they can be.

If any of you use the variety of dating apps out there (and manage to tolerate them for more than five minutes at a time), then by now you're used to the plethora of questions you need to answer: name, age, location, job, religion, politics, etc. And then there are the longer questions, like *Describe your perfect day* and *Are you a pet person?* and, ugh, *What are you looking for in a relationship?*

Don't get me wrong! The answers to those questions are important to know about a partner. But humans are picky, fickle creatures, and sometimes I wish that the questions were a little bit *more* honest so that we could know even sooner (#instant gratification) if this person is worth our very limited time, money, and effort. How is anyone supposed to gauge if the phrase "just want a best friend to go on adventures and Do Life With" means that you're meant to be (let alone gauge what that oft-seen phrase *actually* means)? We need better questions, such as, but not limited to:

- What time do you go to bed, and do you care if I'm under the covers by the time it hits 9:30, moisturized and in fuzzy socks?

- Do you know your sun sign, moon sign, and rising sign? You know what, better yet, go ahead and tell me your Mercury, Venus, and Mars signs as well. Just to be safe.
- Please rate your top five favorite dog breeds.
- In the grand scheme of things, you will not be my top priority (that goes to my family and friends, job, and dog). How do you feel about that?
- Do you care if I play the same new Lizzo single over and over until I know all of the words? (There is only one correct answer.)
- How often do you clean your bathroom? Be honest. (Follow-up question for an appropriate time: How do you feel about the equal division of house labor?)
- On a scale of one to ten, how willing would you be to watch my favorite period drama with me when I'm sick?
- How social are you? What I mean is, how often do you go Out and when you do, what time are you home by? How often would you want me to accompany you?

WHAT YOUR FAVORITE 1990s CHILDREN'S CARTOON SAYS ABOUT YOUR EXPECTATIONS IN RELATIONSHIPS

Will the nostalgia for the '90s ever go away? It can get annoying to be constantly reminded of the past (and that time marches on in only one direction and you can never go back!), but it's hard to cast blame—after all, what's not to like about an era defined by lots of comfy flannel plaid, sunflowers, economic prosperity, and boy bands?

It's been said that Disney has given people unrealistic expectations about love, but what about the absolute bonkers television cartoons we consumed just as frequently? Rumor has it that showrunners at Nickelodeon, in particular, where the vast majority of these cartoons aired, had very little oversight of what they created, so today some of their shows would more likely be considered more appropriate for adults than kids. That's not to say that all the '90s cartoons were weird—PBS was incredibly wholesome, and (daytime) Cartoon Network was, hit-or-miss with appropriate content. Like a lot of things in life, there was a huge spectrum and we were exposed to *all of it.*

Millennials *have* to have been affected by the weird shit they saw as small children, and it's probably manifested in ways of which you're barely aware, such as in relationships. Sure, Disney might have the edge up on chaste kisses and patriarchal values, but when it came to actual interactions between characters? Daytime cartoon television had them beat.

Hey Arnold!: You saw Helga and Arnold's dynamic and immediately knew that you had come aboard the enemies-to-friends-to-lovers express train and there was no getting off! Helga's constant taunts to Arnold's face because she couldn't deal with facing her feelings publicly (a trait that we all know she inherited from her gruff father, #daddyissues, *amiright?*) while mooning over him and her creepy bubble-gum shrine in her room (*how* did she manage to keep all of the roaches and rats away?) were something that we didn't know how much we would come to relate to given time. Yay, repressing feelings and vulnerability!

While the outdated adage "little boys pulling on little girls' pigtails means they like them" was flipped here, perhaps this still gave you some unrealistic, and probably unhealthy, expectations as to what love looks like. At its worst, your idea of a dream partner is someone who expresses affection through constant scowling and makes comments about the shape of your head, aka Helga to Arnold. If this is your Thing, then far be it from me to kink-shame! But perhaps a better way to go is to look for a partner who balances you out and makes you want to be a better person, the way Arnold does for Helga.

Doug: Oh, Doug. Sensitive, journal-writing Doug. We stan a man who understands and practices healthy outlets for processing his emotions! You took one look at that sparsely covered head and knew that you had found your ideal. What can't Doug do? He writes, he's a musician ("Bangin' on a Trash Can" is still a, well, *banger*, and no one can tell me otherwise), and he's such a good Dog Dad to his pup, Porkchop. Sounds like a perfect guy!

. . . Except for the fact that he's obsessed with his first love, Patti Mayonnaise, and to be honest, he probably always will be. Such devotion is admirable, but this likely means that you've fallen for the ideal person, barring their emotional un-availability. Like all of us reading this section, they're stuck in the past and have no inclination to ever get out of it toward a much better future. No matter how perfect this person seems, if they can't ever see past their ex to you, then you need to tell them to "Beet" it (why is "Killer Tofu" stuck in my head?).

Rugrats: There was no blatant romance in *Rugrats*—thank God, because this is a show about literal babies—but if *Rugrats* is your favorite show, don't think you're off the hook here! Basically, this indicates that you're attracted to people who have a youthful energy—if you're someone who tends to be more uptight and serious, this could be a good thing to balance you out and make sure you slow down and enjoy life's simple pleasures. However, if you're also someone who's a little immature, this could be *too much* of a good thing. Sure, the idea of playing all day, interspersed with lots of naps and cookies, sounds like you're living your absolute best life. Unfortunately, reality will hit harder than Angelica's stinging barbs (I would also advise that if you're attracted to anyone who has any qualities that resemble Angelica's, you should run . . . far away and immediately).

Arthur: Adult you is super into John Legend, and this is probably why! Just kidding, that's a cop-out analysis (although I'm right, aren't I?). Hate to break it to you, but if your favorite TV show was *Arthur*, it's likely that your taste in romantic partners runs a little basic and boring. This isn't just an opinion, it's fact! Sorry, *Arthur*, because you ran on PBS and not Nickelodeon, you had a very limited chance for weirdness, or really much of a distinguishable personality at all. This isn't necessarily a bad thing! Listen, you need the easygoing vanilla shows to balance out the *Rocko's Modern Life* and *Aaahh!!! Real Monsters* craziness, and that sort of complementary energy applies to relationships as well. If your fave show was *Arthur*, it means that you value stability, morality, and someone who really likes going to the library, all of which are great attributes in a partner. But your Arthur-esque love definitely needs a partner who gets them out of their PBS shell—they need a little less NPR and a little more rock and roll, you know what I mean?

The Powerpuff Girls: Speaking of complementary energies, if *The Powerpuff Girls* was your favorite show, it means you want a partner who's made of sugar and spice and everything nice—wait, no, you don't, that's what you want out of an excellent snickerdoodle cookie. I'm not here to tell you that there's a specific Powerpuff Girl who is your type—a coura-geous leader, a snarky rebel, or a sweet angel—but rather that what you're looking for is a teammate, a true partner who you can rely on when things get tough. Deadbeats and scrubs need not apply here; serious candidates only, because you don't waste time on those who can't pull their weight and aren't willing to work hard to make sure your relationship is as strong and stable as the city of Townsville.

The Magic School Bus: You knew it was a good day in sci-ence class if you got to watch an episode of this because it meant you got to learn something fun and new. I bet you were the type to watch a bunch of these when you got home, and supplement it with reading the latest installment of *Magic Tree House*. If you think I'm making fun of you, I'm not, because learning new things is *awesome*, and you're probably attracted to people who are also intellectually minded, or at the very least, curious and open to new things and new ideas (either that, or you're really into Ms. Frizzle, which, you know what? Is absolutely fair). Just make sure you're either as committed to going down their rabbit hole of knowledge-seeking as they are, or are able to pull them back from the abyss when they need to come up for air. Hey, I can't say I blame you: the absentminded professor thing is pretty cute, and a passion for knowledge is beyond hot. Just make sure *you're* the subject of their latest study. Wink, wink, glasses nudge.

Recess: As a good kid who didn't like to cause trouble (have people be mad at me and potentially not like me?! Absolutely not—need to avoid that nightmare at all costs), *Recess* functioned almost like a fantasy for me to see the harmless prank antics of a group of close friends who seemingly didn't care that they were constantly getting in trouble with the scowly Miss Finster. Throughout it all, T. J., Gretchen, Mikey, Spinelli, Vince, and Gus were inseparable and loyal no matter what.

If *Recess* was your favorite show, you're looking for someone who's incredibly loyal, sure, but what's more important is that they fit in with your friends. You take friendships very seriously—the Spice Girls' "Wannabe" is probably still one of your all-time played songs (not that I blame you; it still goes hard). You're pretty flexible in terms of what kind of partner you want, but if your friends don't like them, that's a major red flag. You trust their judgments implicitly and are sure that if there's something they don't like, then this person isn't worth keeping around. To that I say, the opinions of friends are always valuable, but in the end you have to trust your own gut.

Ren & Stimpy: You're a freaky-deaky, and you know it. Enough said.

Here's the thing: no one's here to police behavior and social niceties, technically (we're here to make gentle fun of it, really). *But* wouldn't it be nice if everyone could just, I don't know, be adults and *behave* at weddings/family gatherings? (Okay, granted, they might be less interesting, but in turn they'd also probably be less nerve-racking, so I think it's a decent trade-off.)

This section isn't about the basic etiquette one practices at a wedding that I hope we all already know (such as: RSVP on time, don't get wasted, adhere to the dress code, don't wear white, etc.) but rather more nuanced, modern social cues that, man, you *really* wish your aunt Carol and other boomer relatives would keep in mind. You like talking with them and catching up, but not if it always includes their cringe-inducing private questions. Show them this list if you dare (maybe after a few cocktails?) and hope for the best:

- Don't pester the bride or groom about when they plan on having kids, in any capacity, joke or not. They aren't just broodmares and studs! Let them enjoy their wedding! Your question isn't well-meaning, it's invasive.

- Please switch to white wine toward the end of the night instead of sticking with red, especially if you're prone to clumsiness and stumbling while intoxicated. That $5,000 wedding dress doesn't need your sloppy wine stains on it.

- Don't ask any single relatives why they're single. Additionally, don't ask any relatives who are in relationships "when it will be their turn." They either want to be married, don't care about being married, and/or are tired of being asked. What answer are you expecting, actually? Perhaps you think it's just something "fun to say" and it's "harmless," but truly, it's not!

- Do not complain loudly about your issues with the food, drinks, venue, decor, music, and/or dress. Even if any of your criticism has some truth to it, people worked very hard (and spent a *lot* of money, no doubt) on this event. If you must complain, wait until you're in the privacy of your car/home surrounded by trusted people!

- For the love of all that is holy (and all that isn't), don't ask anyone, single or otherwise, about their ex that you met that one time at the family Christmas party. Please. I beg you. No one wants to talk about them. Ever. *Ever*.

- Discussing the physical appearance of anyone, especially if they or anyone they know could possibly hear it, is an absolute no-no! Again, wait until you're alone in your car with trusted people if you have to be a monster, or just don't do it at all! Write it down in your diary and throw it out to sea.

- Please, Aunt Carol, restrain yourself from bringing out your Tupperware and hoarding leftover food. You're not being sneaky, I promise. Everyone can see you.

HALLOWEEN COSTUME IDEAS
FOR A SINGLE PERSON

Who else misses the simple days of childhood Halloween, when your main worry was trying to convince your mom to spend a horrific amount of money on a Party City costume so you could be the coolest kid in class for a day? Halloween candy was a God-given right, and you were safely tucked into bed, warm and asleep, by 10 p.m. Halloween in your twenties and thirties is more like starting out the night cute and dressed up and excited, but at some point during the night it all devolves into a drunken, hot mess.

Worse still is that somehow Halloween has become something of a *romantic* holiday, in which couples' costumes are meticulously planned and entered into contests and flaunted at parties. It's like, "Is *no* holiday sacred these days? Is the only nonromantic holiday, like . . . Easter?" It's too awful to consider. Group costumes are still flourishing, thank God, but it seems like no one truly values the individual costume anymore. Finding the perfect combination of something culturally relevant and clever or even just a little bit sexy (without buying something that just has the word *sexy* in front of it, ugh) is more stressful than it should be!

That said, here are some starting places for evergreen costume ideas (that can also be good for any nonthemed costume party as well):

- **Woman in a Hallmark Movie:** Put on your smart but most generic work clothes, get a blowout of loose waves, and put on pretty but nonthreatening makeup. Carry around a planner and a purse, and say things like, "I'm just a city girl coming to the country to close down this inn, and any cute lumberjack countrymen can get out of my way! Nothing will stop me!"

- **Catwoman:** Buy cat-printed leggings and a T-shirt and you're an homage to both a crazy cat lady and the superhero (villain?) Catwoman.

- **Legally Blonde:** Put on a blond wig if you don't come by it naturally, then print out a fake Legal Certificate to wear around your neck. Dress in a pink lawyer-y suit if you'd like to seal the deal!

- **Table for One:** Get a cardboard box and cut a hole in it for you to step into—ideally the box should be snug around your hips to hold up. Find an old tablecloth to drape around you and the box, and hot-glue plastic or paper cutlery to it. Is it funny? Is it sad? Who can say! But it is clever.

- **Fleabag:** Pick out a flyblack jumpsuit, curl your hair or don a short curly wig, and then apply and smear bright red lipstick and mascara on your face à la Phoebe Waller-Bridge. Carry around a bottle of champagne to complete the look—the best part about this is that you can skip straight to looking like a bit of a hot mess right off the bat! Controlled chaos.

- **Old Maid:** Why not lean into this? You can either make it genuinely funny or horrifying or both: get a maid costume—you can make it as sexy or as unsexy as you want—and top it off with makeup that ages you to your desired level of crone, and utilize other little touches, like reading glasses, a cane, a gray wig, and any other mannerisms your grandmother or aunts adopt.

VI.

Let's Never Do This Again

There are times when you want to be sociable, and there are so many other times when you don't. There are some events that are tolerable, and some that are probably on par with the seventh circle of hell. Hopefully, the latter can either be a) avoided or b) infrequent, but if not, here are some ways to make them better.

You're not quite sure how you ended up here, in a hotel ball-room/overpriced trendy bar/corner of your old cafeteria, at your high school reunion. Alone. You were *adamant* that you would never attend one of these unless you had a hot piece of arm candy. You swore that you would rather scoop out your own eyeballs with a grapefruit spoon than see these class-mates again. And yet!!! Here you are, drinking a watered-down rum and Coke and wishing that you, too, to quote legendary icon Cher, could "turn back time" if only to stop yourself from giving in to your best friend who said that this would be *so fun, Melissa,* and *remember those people from high school whose Instagrams we follow and thought that it would be fun to see again? Maybe they'll be there!* Spoiler: You thought it would be fun while you were *wine drunk,* and they *aren't* here, and your BFF has ditched you to go make out with the boy-from-tenth-grade-English-who-got-away. Standing in a corner by yourself reminds you too much of homecom-ing dances of yore, so there's nothing to do but mingle with people who knew you at the most awkward period of both of your lives. At least make it interesting by indulging in a drinking game: as the night goes on, at least you'll have alcohol and increasing levels of intoxication to help endure the following remarks and events (take a drink at every one you come across):

- "You haven't changed at all since high school!"/"You look so different!"

- Your high school ex shows off their current significant other and you have no one to shove back in their face.

- People tell you how old their kid is in months, even though "two and a half" would have been fine.

- You are mistaken for a completely different person (who is also single).

- You took one shot too many when you saw your old nemesis because you had no one to stop you.

- Someone tells you a "remember when?" story you were not present for or don't remember.

- You find out about a high school–era scandal you never knew about but have no one to share the hot gossip with.

- Someone shows up wearing their old letterman jacket.

- Finish your drink: Someone shows you a baby picture and the baby is not cute.

- Someone brings up your embarrassing yearbook "most likely to."

- Two people who used to date each other show up with SOs who also used to date each other.

- Of the three Kelly/Kelley/Kellis you can't remember which is mean, which is boring, and which is sad, and who would be worse to endure for five minutes in the bathroom line.

- You're halfway through making up an extravagant lie about how fabulous your life is before you realize you don't have a partner-in-crime to back up said lie.

- There is no one present worthy to have an "after-party" with.

Ah, it's that time of year again: the winter holidays. Every time Thanksgiving rolls around, excitement and dread are felt in equal measure. (Pro: Mom's homemade pumpkin pie. Con: sitting next to Aunt Carol for two hours while she grills you on every aspect of your life.) But with the end of Thanksgiving comes the beginning of the Christmas/Hanukkah/Kwanzaa season, which means: Holiday Card Season.

Perhaps more of our parents' generation indulges in holiday cards, but this is one tradition that millennials haven't killed off yet. Don't get me wrong! At its core, the idea of

holiday cards is a nice one: a way to let loved ones who you don't see often know what you've been up to throughout the year. But it can also quickly devolve into a Bragging Session, and an inadvertent way for people to feel shitty about what they Don't Have in their lives—basically what I'm trying to say is, were holiday cards the OG Instagram?!

Whether or not you yourself send holiday cards, it would be nice if everyone could just be honest about both the good and bad of their lives!

Dear College Friend Who I Haven't Seen in Seven Years,

Happy Holidays! I was so thrilled to receive little Emilynne's (did I get that spelling right?) birth announcement. We should totally meet up for a drink and catch-up once you're at the point where you're getting more than two hours of sleep a night :)

My year has been as fine as it can be in this political and economic climate (haha! . . . But really). My promotion at work has been delayed yet again, due to supposed budget restraints and the fact that my boss really wants me to do "something out of the ordinary" in my job to really "prove" that I'm "committed," whatever that means. I guess working ten-hour days isn't enough! Haha! I've decided to start job hunting, and updating my resumé has been more of a challenge than I thought. Who knows what I've been doing the past several years at this job! Not me, when I get down to it.

As for my love life, which I know you're very

interested in, since it's all you ask me about when we text, it's . . . typical, I guess (not that you would know, since you've been with Dave since sophomore year! Well, except for that time he broke up with you so he could be single during his study abroad trip, but we don't have time to get into all of that). I am on several dating apps, and the odds are good, but the goods . . . are odd. I think my longest "relationship" lasted two months, and honestly, that was probably because one of us was out of town for a good chunk of it (coincidentally, why we ended it). But you never know! I guess I'll just keep going, because what other choice do I have? Meet someone organically? As our mutual friend mournfully said at our college graduation, "We'll never be around this many single guys our age ever again." Little did we know how right she was!

My dog, Pepper, however, is still a delight, thank God. She had exactly one vet scare, and that was because she ate my shoelace and it ended up stuck in her stomach. That bill was horrific, but I don't have any children, so I guess if that's where my money goes, that's where it goes! I had to wrestle her into that bow tie, but I think it looks cute! The pet photographer I hired kept calling Pepper a "good boy," but I let it slide because the societal concept of a gender binary is a helluva drug, and I didn't feel like getting into my usual lecture of why policing gender among animals is especially strange.

I went on exactly one vacation to Miami and

although I had a great time, I was incredibly sunburnt for a good chunk of it, hence why there is no photographic evidence on this card or even an Instagram selfie. Your yearly trip to Aspen looked fun, though!

My friends are my saving grace. There's a group of us called the Brunch Bunch (we try different brunch spots around the city) and we've found some great places throughout the year. At some point (I don't quite remember when, to be honest), we created a side Instagram where we rate the taste and strength of different mimosas and bloody Marys. It's called @daydrinkersinthecity, with captions of varying length and grammatical quality. My grandma somehow found the account (I think my annoying cousin Sheila ratted me out) and now thinks I'm an alcoholic, but oh, well!

What else? The usual that I do every year, I guess (or have I? I barely know how time works anymore. Each month feels like its own year). I've devoured several Netflix shows and HBO series, and have made minimal-to-medium progress on my To Be Read book list. I go to the gym maybe twice a week, which I consider to be pretty good, and I try to take homemade salads for lunch to work to save money and eat healthier, although I'm bored to tears just typing about eating them.

Anyway, that's me! Happy Holidays, and hope you're doing well.

Xoxo—

FAKE IT TILL YOU MAKE IT: FAKING YOUR WAY THROUGH CONVERSATIONS ABOUT POPULAR TV SHOWS AND MOVIES YOU'VE NEVER SEEN BEFORE

We've all been there: You're at a party or a work function and everyone's talking about that Thing, either the latest streaming craze or something considered "iconic" in all of modern pop culture, and you have no idea what they're talking about. You probably genuinely meant to see it, but without having a significant other to share the TV with (which, to be honest, is pretty great), you only are watching what you want to watch, which is basically reruns of *New Girl*. Unfortunately, this is one of those rare instances in which having a partner would be handy, if only so they could take over this particular party conversation for you, but you're alone, so you just have to do your best until you can sneak away.

And sometimes it's perfectly fine not to contribute to a conversation and just listen, and there's nothing shameful about not being caught up on every single thing that's ever happened in pop culture, but if you would rather go with the flow when someone asks your opinion of a show than admit you haven't seen it, to horrified gasps, then this guide is for you.

THE CROWN

- **What You Need to Know:** A historical drama that covers the reign of Queen Elizabeth II, aka Prince William and Harry's grandmother, beginning with her marriage to Philip and eventually ending in modern day. The series will eventually span six seasons, with different actors and actresses filtering in and out every few seasons to account for changing ages and time periods. Despite its name and subject matter, it's shockingly *not* as boring as a History Channel documentary and, if you squint a little bit and take away the posh accents, has some elements of your favorite *Real Housewives* franchise. (Tables aren't being flipped and there are no spray tans, but there *is* catty drama between rich white people who possess a lot of bling. Royals! They're just like us.)

- **Your Contribution to the Conversation:** Because it's rooted in real life (although there's a hefty amount of fictionalization, obviously), it's a little easier to fake this one than others. Popular opinions, however, include that Prince Philip is a dick (fuckbois permeate every social class, like a disease), and that Claire Foy did a great job portraying the young queen. Olivia Colman, who took over for her, is the perfect queen, and you can just say something like how you worship at her throne.

GAME OF THRONES

- **What You Need to Know:** People could be talking about either the HBO series or the books (There are *books*? you might be thinking in horror. There are, they're huge, I've never read them.), but it's most likely the former. Just so you know, though, *Game of Thrones* refers to the TV series and the technical reference for the books is *A Song of Ice and Fire*, by George R. R. Martin. The book series is not finished, but the TV series (as I'm sure you heard over and over during the course of 2019) is. Both follow the machinations of royal families in the fictional Seven Kingdoms of Westeros as they battle it out to be its ruler and sit upon the Iron Throne. There's court intrigue, romance, battles, secrets, hidden identities, and more. And since George R. R. Martin is a li'l freak, there's also incest, a crap-ton of violence, some frozen zombies (called White Walkers), a crap-ton of sex, and just, like, people getting killed in basically every way imaginable. If someone starts talking about the Red Wedding, don't ask questions, just nod and grimace and hope they don't go into details. Trust me.

- **Your Contribution to the Conversation:** When people say the last season and finale of the show were bad, just agree with them. It's not worth it to try to have a controversial opinion. People who are really into *Game of Thrones* can drone on about it for so long they give people who drone on about their kids a run for their money. If people ask you who your favorite family (or House) was, you can play it safe and say the Starks, but if you want to be a little more devious, you can say the Lannisters, especially Cersei; you could sympathize with a woman who wanted power in a male-dominated world and really loved her wine. Otherwise, sit back and sip your own glass of wine.

GILMORE GIRLS

- **What You Need to Know:** I would bet there's a good chunk of your friends who were (or still are) obsessed with this show, but unfortunately, they're not here right now to cover for you, so you need to do your best and muddle through so people aren't thinking you grew up under a rock. Current single mom/former teen mom Lorelai Gilmore lives with her teenaged daughter, Rory Gilmore, in a charming small town in Connecticut called Stars Hollow. Lorelai is outgoing and spunky, Rory is quiet and bookish, but they both engage in rapid-fire witty exchanges, usually laden with pop culture references, both obvious and obscure. It's banter that's truly the stuff of every aspiring-pretentious teen's dream. Rory's goal is to go to Harvard, and to do that she needs to go to a good high school, so Lorelai swallows her pride and asks her snobby, estranged, old-money parents for help to pay for Rory to go to private school (man, must be so nice to have that sort of financial safety net!). What follows are several seasons of mixing old worlds and new, and lots of romances for both Lorelai and Rory. Although this series has been officially over since 2007, there was a miniseries sequel *A Year in the Life* that ran on Netflix in 2016, with rumors that there may be more installations, so we haven't seen the last of the Gilmores!

- **Your Contribution to the Conversation:** People have very strong Opinions on *Gilmore Girls*, but if you want to get through this conversation relatively unscathed, here are the most popular ones you can recite to your fellow partygoers, which, unsurprisingly, have to do with their love interests: Rory's first boyfriend, Dean, is trash. Her college boyfriend, Logan, is also trash. Her second boyfriend, Jess, was once trash but is now

Perfect and they are Made for Each Other (He likes books! She likes books! Can I make it any more obvious?). To be honest, I really think Rory could use a book like this one—she generally has awful taste in men and should probably be single for a *long* while! As for Lorelai's boyfriends, they're all basically irrelevant except Luke, local diner owner and slow-burn love interest. Oh, and Stars Hollow is *so cute*, how *fun would it be to live there*?! *Cue squealing.*

PRIDE AND PREJUDICE

- **What You Need to Know:** Maybe a good chunk of this guide has been redundant for you, sci-fi/fantasy/superhero fan that you are, and what you really need is a guide on Jane Austen movies and other period dramas because your friends are nuts over them and you just aren't. That is totally valid. Arguably the most popular/well-known period drama adaptation is Jane Austen's *Pride and Prejudice,* which is the equivalent of a romantic dramedy about Elizabeth Bennet and Mr. Darcy, who initially loathe each other but end up falling in love. While I can't say for sure if this concept originated with Jane A., she certainly is the Patron Saint of the Enemies-to-Lovers trope that many of us find so delicious. Mr. Darcy is seen as the quintessential romantic hero, but unlike some other problematic faves, his reputation is earned. Although he begins as a judgmental, aristocratic snob, he ultimately is a loyal, noble man with integrity who—and this is how you know this book is fiction—*listens to Elizabeth's criticisms and* *undergoes change to become a better man.* In short: Jane Austen did what the other girls couldn't do!! Real-life men take note, because this book has been out for two hundred years and here most of you are, still being awful when you had this man to be your guide.

- **Your Contribution to the Conversation:** What is probably being discussed are the various films, particularly the 1995 version versus the 2005 version. There's usually a lot of Discourse about the two versions and which is better, and to be honest, who cares. They're both great in their own ways, with equally dreamy eye candy to keep you occupied: the 1995 BBC version stars Colin Firth and the 2005 adaptation stars Keira Knightley. Or just say you like the 1995 version because you like a wet Colin Firth (I won't tell you any more details than that, you just have to watch the movie yourself!)—I highly doubt you'll get any disagreements there.

STAR WARS

- **What You Need to Know:** Oh, boy. Whew, where do we start? Best to keep it simple: it's a sci-fi space opera with Carrie Fisher kicking ass and making out with Harrison Ford and a bunch of sequels that range from fair to god-awful that have cool fight scenes (but not enough Harrison Ford, although to be fair, there's *never* enough Harrison Ford in anything). There are nine movies, known as "episodes," total in this sci-fi space opera. The entire series follows the Skywalker family, with Luke Skywalker, played by Mark Hamill, as the main protagonist. Carrie Fisher plays Princess Leia and Harrison Ford plays good-hearted scoundrel Han Solo. It's a classic good-versus-evil scenario, with Luke representing the Good Guys, or the Jedi, which are basically telekinetic, strong religious warriors who battle against the Dark Side, aka the Sith, who are their evil counterparts. A lot of this is done with a lot of cool fight scenes in outer space, so yes, this series is basically just ninja-wizards in space.

- **Your Contribution to the Conversation:** A lot of this conversation can honestly be handled by whatever passionate fans are in your group, but if push comes to shove, stick to this: *The Empire Strikes Back (Episode V)* is the best movie of the bunch, the prequels are garbage (the name Jar Jar Binks should be avoided at all costs), the follow-up trilogy is fine, at best, and Princess Leia is a badass supreme. Fair warning: you might have people argue with you on the last one, but rest assured that they're wrong. I'll say it again because it bears repeating: she got to *command an army and make out with Harrison Ford.* Double down and just say there's nothing they can say that will change your mind. It's fun to see any misogynistic fanboys lose their minds.

STAR TREK

- **What You Need to Know:** There have been many iterations of *Star Trek* movies, television shows, animated series, etc., but the original started in the 1960s, with good ol' William Shatner as Captain James T. Kirk of the USS *Enterprise* and Leonard Nimoy as Spock, his alien first officer. Episodic and ridiculous a good chunk of the time, nevertheless the series, created by Gene Roddenberry, is considered to be revolutionary in many ways. Since then there have been spin-off movies and series, with the most recent film series being the "reboots" with Chris Pine as Kirk and Zachary Quinto as Spock, although it's been several years since the last one was made. Fun Fact: There is a *lot* of excellent eye candy in this franchise. A young Will Shatner was *hot*, Zoe Saldana wears supershort skirts that show off her legs, and one movie even features a small cameo by Chris Hemsworth! Two Hollywood Chrises for the price of one; who can pass that up?

- **Your Contribution to the Conversation:** It really depends on which series the group is talking about (there are *many*), but you can say something like how you hope there's a new movie being made with Chris Pine, although you can't stand the light flares that J.J. Abrams uses in them (seriously, sometimes I need to put on sunglasses when I watch those movies, although of course I take them off anytime Chris Pine is shirtless). You can turn it back on them and ask what they think of the new series, *Star Trek: Discovery* and *Picard*, and that'll get them going for ages. Oh, and if you really want to rile up the narrow-minded homophobes who might be in your conversation, just keep insisting that Kirk and Spock are gay for each other. It'll drive them nuts. "They're in love," you insist. "Gays in space! Gay rights!"

WHAT AM I GETTING MYSELF INTO: AN EVENT'S ANATOMY

So you got an invite to a party. Yay! It's nice to be thought of, right? Or maybe you don't care about that kind of thing at all because you don't suffer from FOMO, in which case, I salute you, because that shit is incurable. But before you say YES, stop and think about what this event might entail. Skimming the five W's, checking your calendar, and RSVP-ing immediately is a reckless, if not downright foolish, idea. This might sound weird, but conjure up both your ninth-grade English teacher *and* your inner wilderness scout, because it's always best to do some critical analysis before you know what you're getting into, and how you can then prepare for it.

Perhaps you feel I'm overreacting, but think about your best friend's/roommate's/sister's birthday party and how you thought it'd be a great time, because, hey! you love that person and they're awesome and so their party must be, too. But planning a party is a delicate business, and instead of looking great and feeling great the whole night, you ended up with running mascara, a broken right shoe, and were $150 in the hole (and that's not even mentioning the god-awful hangover you woke up with the day after).

So think before you speak, and if you need help, you can always phone a friend (but don't phone the friend whose party it is, obviously):

Yo

What's up?

I need some advice

Hit me

Remember my friend, Vicky? I got an invite to her birthday party & am deciding whether or not I should go

I'm guessing you're free that night

Yup. I guess I could lie to get out of it, but I hate doing that

And it could be fun? Sometimes I have fun at her parties

True, but aren't they so elaborate? And time-consuming. And expensive

Yeah . . .

Ok, break down this party for me then

Ok

So she wants to start off at that new bar downtown, Foxtrot

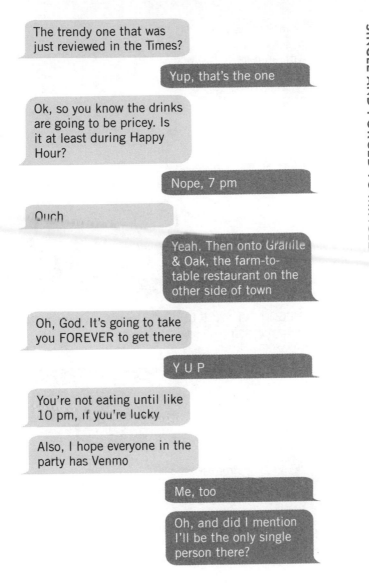

The trendy one that was just reviewed in the Times?

Yup, that's the one

Ok, so you know the drinks are going to be pricey. Is it at least during Happy Hour?

Nope, 7 pm

Ouch

Yeah. Then onto Granite & Oak, the farm-to-table restaurant on the other side of town

Oh, God. It's going to take you FOREVER to get there

Y U P

You're not eating until like 10 pm, if you're lucky

Also, I hope everyone in the party has Venmo

Me, too

Oh, and did I mention I'll be the only single person there?

Yeah, unless Vicky tries to set you up again with another one of her boyfriend's fraternity brothers

PLEASE DON'T REMIND ME

How likely is it that she'll try again?

Pretty likely!! She'll want to make sure I'm "having fun" aka have a dance partner for when we go to that dance club, Flit, after

OH GOD, A DANCE CLUB?! There's gonna be a cover & everything, I bet

Yeah, so if Finance Bro #4 could cover it, that would be great

sigh she means well

Ok, so to summarize: the entire party consists of non-subsidized drinks, a car to dinner, dinner itself, a car to the club, club cover, probably more drinks, then a car home?

Yeah, I think that's everything

And you probably won't get home until like, 3 am

. . . Yeah

So forget going to the gym or meal prepping or doing laundry the next day. You're just going to be in bed, recovering

Ok, rude!

I'm not being rude, I'm being realistic! Isn't that why you asked me for advice?

Which I'm now regretting!

Lol sounds like the only thing you'll be regretting is going to this party

How pissed would Vicky be if you didn't go? Like, you don't have to LIE per se, just say vaguely that you can't come but will make it up to her with a nice dinner just the two of you?

That could work, but IDK, I feel guilty not just going because I don't want to . . .

Ok, here's my advice:

Maybe she would take a dinner with just the two of you better than you trying to weasel your way into only going to part of this all-night extravaganza

You're right, she'd be pissed if I didn't stay for the whole thing

Or you could suck it up and go to the whole thing

Because sometimes being a good friend means doing whatever your BFF wants to make them happy, and sometimes it means recognizing your own limits and finding another way to celebrate that will make them happy and not completely wreck your weekend/make you broke, hungover, and miserable. Your call!

You're right

UGH, you're right and I hate it

But you still come to me for advice! LOL

Good luck!

Thanks, either way I need it

VII.

F*** This, Actually

Being an adult is hard; playing nice even in the face of mind-numbingly boring events and invasive personal questions is even harder. Sometimes you're only thirty seconds away from literally running away, packing up your essentials and scurrying off to the woods to be a hermit. I'm not saying that's a terrible idea, but don't you think you'd miss running water and electricity? Sometimes a Pity Party is a good enough catharsis to keep those hermit dreams at bay a little longer.

To quote everyone's favorite scientist, Bill Nye, consider the following:

- If a typical family gathering lasts three hours and you have four nosy aunts, how many times will you be set up per half hour per relative? (Other factors to solve for: the one aunt who is relentless in her questioning, the one aunt who steamrolls over any answers you give, the one aunt who gets easily distracted, the one aunt who forgets which niece you are.)

- Your best friend and her husband have become *those people* and thrown a gender reveal party (theme on the banner: "Stud or Starlet?"). If you spend x amount of minutes having the gender binary thrown at you relentlessly, at what y decibel will you finally scream?

- Let's say your second cousin Natalie shows up late to your great-grandfather's funeral wearing all white, including a tight tank top, ripped jeans, and brand-new Air Jordans. Her baby daddy and crying, grubby toddler are with her. Taking all factors into account, how many times over the course of the wake, church service, reception, and family only after-dinner will you be asked when you're going to settle down and have a nice family like Natalie?

- Tonight's mandatory quarterly office party is also tripling as your boss's engagement celebration and your coworker's baby shower. Considering the pitying looks you're being given for your constant singledom, how many glasses of cheap wine do you need to consume per sixty minutes in order to achieve the optimal loose buzz while still being able to sober up quickly enough to hightail it out of there as soon as the party's over? (You are not being paid overtime.)

- If your stepbrother Jeremy has been married three times before the age of forty to women named Keely, Kylie, and Kayleigh, what are the odds that you are definitely going to call his current wife the wrong name?

- It's Holiday/Engagement Season. If your best friend gets engaged on Thanksgiving, your ex on Christmas Day, and your nemesis on New Year's Eve, how likely is it that by Valentine's Day you've deleted all social media apps?

- You're a little tipsy, at home, on a Friday night, and you know what that means: swiping time on various dating apps. If twenty people message you, what percentage of them are in an open relationship and looking for someone to join their throuple; want someone to "go on adventures with," aka a lot of outdoor sporting trips; like to fish; or are on the rebound from a long-term relationship?

FAKE BEAUTY PRODUCTS
FOR EVERY TYPE OF CRISIS

Like a lot of people who've become enamored with/suckered into the Self-Care Scene/Scheme (that is to say, self-care is absolutely a healthy habit that people should embrace in whatever form is meaningful for them, but let's be clear: like many things, Capitalism™ has overtaken it), going to LUSH has become a semiregular staple in my life. Stepping into the fragrance-saturated store, with its black walls, large sinks, and many products, has become a treat in which I indulge during a variety of times: before business trips, after business trips, birthdays (my own and others'), major holidays, stressful weeks, and the list goes on. Whether it's a product that's part of my daily routine or one that's just for Special Occasions/Emergencies only, 80 percent of the time LUSH can cure all woes (and to be clear, this is #not an #ad, I just really like LUSH). Someone get me on the phone with LUSH's CEO, because I have *ideas* for products that could get them all the way to 100 percent:

Memory Dissolve Bath Bomb: Soak in the frothy delights of this eye-catching orange and buttercup-yellow bath bomb when your day has gone so spectacularly wrong that you wish you could forget it—literally! Instead of rehashing it repeatedly in your brain to see what you could have done/said differently or with your therapist, you would really just like to forget that you ever had to endure the period that started with a rude person bumping into you, spilling coffee on your favorite shirt (that you meant to get dry-cleaned for months and finally did, and you were *just* congratulating yourself on being a Responsible Adult!), continued with absolutely *bombing* (see what I did there) your presentation at work, followed up with getting ghosted by that Tinder match who you actually were looking forward to meeting. Just dump this li'l baby in the bath and let it dissolve, along with all of your horrified memories of this day.

Scream Cream: Slather on this calming lotion after enduring people for an excruciating length of time and/or when the mere idea of interacting with another human being makes you want to screech at the top of your lungs. Infused with the soothing extract of Solitude, the healthy dose of the Sense of Peace You Feel After Spending an Entire Weekend in Your Bedroom will do wonders for your sense of patience and tolerance for others. And the best part? It will actually repel people from looking at or speaking to you for a solid twelve hours. You won't be invisible, per se, but you will definitely be left alone if you go out in public. Oh, and there's a little bit of chamomile and oat milk in it—for dry skin, obviously.

Healing Heartbreak Body Scrub: Sometimes when your heart gets broken, it helps to wallow a bit—cry it out, eat some chocolate, go full-on Elle Woods in your breakup misery. And sometimes, you want to get over it as soon as possible. The Healing Heartbreak Body Scrub can help with the latter, at least a little bit! Rub this into your skin after a bad breakup, romantic, platonic, or otherwise, and while it can't heal your broken heart completely, it will help scrub away the memories and feelings you have about that person. Made with a healthy dose of Closure and Hindsight, this is a surefire way to jump-start the process of Moving On.

ASMR Hair Mask: Stressed out? Had a long day? Look no further than the relaxing properties of the ASMR Hair Mask. Massage it into your hair and leave it on as long as you like: immediately you'll start to feeling the "tingling" sensation commonly associated with ASMR, or autonomous sensory meridian response. All of the tension and tiredness will fade away as the mask works its pseudoscientific ASMR magic. Not to mention, when you eventually wash it out your hair will be extra voluminous, too. Win-win!

Energize! Shower Gel: Waking up after your third awful date in a row is hard to do, and people have a variety of coping mechanisms that tend to not be the healthiest for them, like lots of coffee, soda, or caffeine pills with alarming names like Jet-Alert. Lather up with this gel while you're taking your morning shower and feel a rush of energy to jump-start your day! Infused with citrus, Adrenaline, and a smidgen of Insomnia, the effects of this gel linger for ten hours and can get you through any pointless meeting, long commute, or droning co-worker! It's also available in body spray form, perfect to spritz on as an evening boost before a big date or boring dinner party.

TELL ME HOW YOUR LAST RELATIONSHIP ENDED AND I'LL TELL YOU WHICH CHAIN RESTAURANT YOU SHOULD EAT YOUR FEELINGS AT

Before you decide to skip this section, hear me out: Chain restaurants are perfect places to go after a relationship has ended. Once you've gotten tired of takeout and being cooped up in your room, going to a chain restaurant for sustenance is a great next step. Why? Several reasons:

- It gets you out of your house, where you might have been going a little stir-crazy.
- It's not fancy, but it is a step up from takeout and the drive-through, and you'll need to put in some amount of effort, like putting on pants. Baby steps.
- Chain restaurants are the opposite of romantic, so while I'm sure there will be some "date nights," there won't be many and they won't be very gushy, so you can hopefully avoid PDA and romance triggers for a bit.
- Your ex will not be there. Why would your ex be there? They wouldn't be (unless it's their favorite restaurant, in which case, if that's true, then I have more questions).

If you broke up because they cheated on you, go to Red Robin: First of all, screw your ex, because you're amazing, and how dare they cheat on you! Second of all, Red Robin is the best place to go when someone you emotionally depended upon lied to you and betrayed you because Red Robin is the exact opposite: Red Robin is dependable. Red Robin is reliable. Red Robin is solid. When you go into a Red Robin, you know exactly what to expect, no matter which location you go to, no matter if it's been several years since you've set foot in one. The menu rarely changes, or if it does, you can always count on your favorites being there: the strawberry lemonade in the swirly glass; the perfectly cooked steak fries with a healthy sprinkling of the special seasoning blend on them; the rich chocolate milkshakes with the metal tin can on the side. In a world of chaos, we can only be certain of these things: life, death, taxes, and Red Robin.

It you broke up because of long distance, go to Olive Garden: Perhaps this seems counterintuitive, but when a relationship dissolves because of distance, the best thing to do is create even *more* distance by just leaving for a while and getting out of your space. If you're unable to actually do this, then the next best thing to do is to go to Olive Garden and pretend you're in Italy for an hour and a half. Is the fake Tuscan villa decor *authentic* and *convincing*? Absolutely not! But they have a pretty solid happy hour, and you won't feel too guilty about the carbo-loading you're going to do when you devour four servings of the Never Ending Pasta Bowl special, because it *also* comes with unlimited salad! It's the healthiest you've eaten in the weeks post-breakup, and as Oprah once told Lindsay Lohan, that's something to celebrate.

If you broke up because they were a loser, go to Red Lobster: When you finally kick your scrub of an ex to the curb, you need to treat yourself, and that's why you're going to go to the crème de la crème of chain restaurants: Red Lobster. Even if you don't like seafood, at least go and order a large Lobsterita, a margarita the size of your head, and stuff a dozen or two of their delicious cheddar biscuits in your mouth. If you *do* like seafood, get yourself whatever you want, even if it's the lobster itself; since that fool clearly didn't treat you right, you need to treat yourself way better than they ever did. Plus, using a crab cracker to crush the shell is a satisfying and cathartic way to relieve tension.

If you broke up because there was no chemistry, go to TGI Fridays: You wanted to make it work so badly, because they were wonderful and lovely and you always had so much fun when you went out on dates, but unfortunately halfway through one said date you realized that you felt and acted exactly as you did whenever you were with friends, which is to say, completely platonically. That epiphany had you realizing the sex that was perfunctory and fine was never really going to get better, was it, and that it was better to end this thing now rather than drag it out, hoping it would get hotter someday.

But you know what you'll always have amazing chemistry with? Their mozzarella sticks and marinara sauce (if you're lactose intolerant, their chicken strips are bomb, too). Tell me, what's more sensual than cheesy goodness oozing out of a perfectly crisp exterior? Pull a Liz Lemon and work on that night cheese, consoling yourself with the knowledge that one day you will find someone who will do you right.

If you broke up because you fought constantly, go to the Cheesecake Factory: I'll be honest, I originally picked this because of the line in the Drake song, "Why you gotta fight with me at Cheesecake? / You know I love to go there," but after thinking about it, it's actually very fitting that you go to a Cheesecake Factory after this kind of breakup because, like your ex, the Cheesecake Factory is actually mystifying and infuriating. With both, nothing makes sense and you feel so deeply unsettled that you just want to scream.

Maybe you'll try to say that it's not that deep, but what is even happening with the Cheesecake Factory decor? Saying it out loud makes me feel like I'm a time-traveler: Egyptian columns, Victorian siding, fresco ceiling details, southern-style wicker chairs, palm tree accents? It's like a mishmash of every themed restaurant you could ever go to, and that's not even touching the menu. Besides the obvious cheesecake, there are Italian flatbreads, Thai coconut stir fries, enchiladas and tacos, British shepherd's pie, and even tuna ahi poke.

Confront this chaos and work through it, one bread basket at a time. I'm convinced that time and space work differently inside a Cheesecake Factory, and once you leave, you won't be the same person that you were when you arrived—hopefully you've achieved an inner peace that your ex never could've given you.

MELISSA CROCE

Even if your love life isn't on point right now, your liquor game (if you drink) should always be. Sure, the basic cocktails could do the trick if you just want to be buzzed enough to get through the evening, but you deserve more than a watered-down rum and Coke (looking at *you*, awkward high school reunion!). Besides impressing the hell out of everyone you know, these drinks will be yummy enough to brighten any dull and dreadful situation.

Dirty Hornitini

The "horni" part refers to the type of tequila used, but your parents' nosy neighbors who you randomly ran into at the local bar during a visit home don't need to know that! Let them think you live like an extra on *Girls*!

2 ounces tequila (Hornitos Reposado tequila)
1 ounce dry vermouth
½ to 1 ounce olive juice (or olive brine, to taste)
Dash Angostura orange bitters
Garnish: green olive

Pour the ingredients into a cocktail shaker filled with ice. Stir well. Strain into a cocktail glass. Garnish with a single olive on a cocktail pick.

The Devil's Handshake

For situations when you would rather make a deal with the devil than be at this event on your own any longer. Thank Satan for this drink.

For the ginger puree:
1-inch piece fresh ginger
1 teaspoon sugar (optional)

Cut thin slices of fresh ginger and process in a food processor or blender until smooth. Add a teaspoon of sugar, if desired. Place the puree into an ice cube tray and freeze.

For the drink:
1½ ounces tequila
¾ ounce lime juice
½ ounce simple syrup
1 ounce pineapple juice
1 teaspoon ginger puree (see above instructions)
1 egg white

Garnish: lime wedge
½-inch piece fresh ginger (sliced)
1 teaspoon sugar (optional)

Place the drink ingredients in a cocktail shaker and dry shake vigorously. Add ice and shake again. Strain over fresh ice in a highball glass. Garnish with a lime wedge and ginger slices.

Witch Hunt

So you look up your horoscope every day and have recently been getting into palm reading. That doesn't mean you're a witch! *But* if you want to play into that persona, despite your friends' teasing, order this drink. Maybe you'll develop witchy powers that will help you speed up time so you can be done with this night.

1½ ounces Scotch whisky
½ ounce dry vermouth
¼ ounce Strega Liqueur
1 ounce lemonade

Build the ingredients in an old-fashioned glass filled with ice. Stir well.

Screaming Orgasm

Shock all of the conservative busybodies whose invasive questions are getting on your last nerve by ordering this shot! What makes this a *screamer* is the vodka added to the liqueurs. Hopefully that little extra kick will get you through the rest of the evening!

¼ ounce vodka
¼ ounce amaretto liqueur
¼ ounce coffee liqueur
¼ ounce Irish cream liqueur

Pour the ingredients into a cocktail shaker filled with ice. Shake well. Strain into a shot glass.

Red Wine with Ice Cubes

Blend in with the married women in your family with this classic Mom Drink. Maybe this camouflage will hide you long enough for people not to notice your bare left hand and barren womb.

Glass of red wine of your choice
2 to 3 ice cubes

Combine and chug it down before the ice waters down the wine. (Bonus points: Drink with a sympathetic but knowing look on your face as you listen to the other women complain about their husbands and children!)

VIII.

Single, Not Sorry

Here's the thing: no matter what kind of shenanigans you have to endure as a single person—third-wheeling, unwanted matchmaking and meddling, bad blind dates, or suffering through social events alone—there are still so many reasons why being single is awesome, and, in many ways, better *than being in a relationship. Never apologize for being single! Be proud of it.*

SEASONAL ACTIVITIES
WITH A PARTNER VERSUS ALONE

Some people think that the holiday season is the saddest time for single people, but true single people know that *each* season has the potential to be soul-crushingly sad! Luckily, there's no reason to be, because Cute Seasonal Activities done in pairs are actually super overrated and honestly, it's better just to do them alone, or with literally any other person in your life—friends, family, your favorite barista, you name it. Sure, fights between those people can certainly happen, but at least you don't have to go home with them later! Anyone who's said that the warehouse pickup section of IKEA is the place where relationships go to die clearly has never stepped foot near a cutesy outdoor ice-skating rink in December.

SPRING ACTIVITY: HIKING TOGETHER
VERSUS PICNIC IN THE PARK ALONE

- *If You're in a Relationship:* Ah, spring, or as I call it, posthibernation. Time to shake off those hermit habits and reemerge into the world with the sun. Alas, it seems like everyone and their snow-bunny-turned-significant-other are also out there showing that they're still in peak physical fitness, because your Instagram feed is absolutely cluttered with pictures of couples posed together on mountaintops or cliffs or whatever, aglow with both sweat, but most importantly, their Love™. Don't despair, especially if you're viewing those pictures while you're still pantsless, in bed, at 1 p.m. on a Saturday, eating from a bag of chips that was left on your bed the night before after you fell asleep, marathon-watching episodes of *The Good Place* again. What Instagram *isn't* showing you is that those couples most definitely argued about at least one thing, if not multiple things, leading up to those victorious-in-love-and-life pictures:

- ▶ **Where to Hike:** "But, babe," one of them whined to the other, "the *views* are much better at Death Hill Mountain. It's a better backdrop for the Insta."

- ▶ **What to Wear:** "We can't be matchy-matchy, but we should also wear complementary colors" is a sentence that I'm sure was uttered. "Also, one of us can't be in Nike while the other is in Adidas—that's not what a unified house looks like."

- ▶ **How Early to Go:** "But do we *really* need to go at sunrise? Those pictures will end up blurry, anyway."

- ▶ **Which Trail to Take:** Obviously there are those Super Couples who do marathons together and stuff, but let's assume here that most couples have different levels of fitness. The trail that they eventually pick will either bore one person or completely kill the other.

- ▶ **How Fast to Walk:** Besides different fitness levels, let's also assume that their legs and strides vary! Someone is absolutely getting left behind and their faster partner will definitely not notice until much, much later.

Rest assured that after the photos were taken, chosen, filtered, cropped, and posted, the couples made their way back down that mountain in complete and total silence, both vowing internally never to hike with the other person again.

- *If You're Single:* Dust off that yoga mat you've used about three times, because that's good enough to use as a picnic blanket, right? (You wouldn't *dare* use your soft bed blankets—those are precious and you're not a monster.) Pour the bottle of rosé that's been literally chilling in your fridge since the night before into your opaque water bottle so your imbibing can be on the down-low, and stuff your tote bag full of whatever you picked up at Trader Joe's last week.

  Hop a bus or walk to your favorite park, where you know exactly which spot is the best for dog-watching. Maybe you'll read a few chapters of that paranormal hockey romance you downloaded (it was free and the guys on the cover were *hot*, never mind that they're Photoshopped to the gills) while drinking and texting some of the most outlandish lines to your friends. If you're *really* lucky, an enthusiastic dog might wander over and you can flirt with its cute owner while they apologize profusely.

  You end up falling asleep, and maybe you're a little sunburnt when you wake up (despite the moisturizer with SPF that I *know* you put on earlier, right?), but once the redness fades a little you know you've set yourself up for a solid base tan to start off the warm seasons with. Maybe you Insta-storied a shot of your picnic spot with whatever's been dubbed the preemptive song of the summer with a pithy little caption, or you didn't and life goes on. Either way, good job!!

SUMMER ACTIVITY: ROAD TRIP TOGETHER VERSUS BEACH DAY WITH FRIENDS

- *If You're in a Relationship:* Going on an extended trip is a bold move for any relationship, platonic or not, and going on a road trip is *especially* bold: stuck in a small space that you can't escape for hours on end, in which you're subjected to someone else's particular car habits, and, even worse, they're subjected to *yours*? The idea of being known has never been more mortifying, I'm sure. But hey, the Insta of that Starbucks cup with the dashboard and accompanying sunrise in the background on day one, hour one, is too good to pass up, am I right?

  If both people are Type A (meticulously planned playlists, bathroom breaks, estimated spots of heavy traffic, and snacks and backup car supplies all in a freshly washed, dusted, and vacuumed car) or Type B (half-reliable USB cord for a phone playlist, an over-reliance on the Waze app, and the only snacks are leftover Cheetos from the night before stuffed in between the various coats, shoes, take-out menus, and plastic or reusable grocery bags that clutter the backseat), then that couple will probably get through their trip relatively unscathed. But if that couple is a mixture of the two, then whooo, buddy, get ready for World War III, as taken place in one 2012 Barcelona-red Toyota Prius.

  Everything from the playlists (has someone been

meticulously curating a Spotify playlist for weeks, only to have every selection scoffed at by their partner?) to the amount and timing of bathroom breaks (the best and cleanest places to pee were absolutely researched by one person, while the other is fine with playing rest-stop roulette—and couldn't they have gone when they stopped for gas thirty minutes ago, anyway?) is debated, and things only go downhill from there! Soon, the reason for said road trip will be called into question (if they're headed to visit someone's family and home-town, someone's high school ex will most definitely be brought up and weaponized; if it's to a particular vacation spot, one person will undoubtedly declare that they never wanted to go there in the first place). By the time they get to where they're going, it'll be a miracle if they haven't broken up, let alone arrived with minimal tension. Resentment levels will skyrocket, just like the price of gas, no matter how fuel efficient that Prius is. To those brave enough to road-trip with someone they're not legally bound to (or even if they are!), good luck, because you're going to need it.

- *If You're Single:* In many ways, summer can be absolutely terrible: every pore on your body makes itself known by *secreting* liquid, like you're a frog (no offense to frogs), and suddenly everyone wants to socialize, like, *all the time*: barbecues, rooftop happy hours, late-night barhopping, movies in the park . . . And sure, in theory that all sounds great, but it seems to come all at once, and your glorious visions of napping in the sun are gone with the spring. But! You know what's fun? Beach (or pool, or lake) days with friends.

Picture it: you and a select group of friends round up old and new copies of *The New Yorker* or *Cosmo* or that one book you've been meaning to read for about six months now; pack some beer, chips, and sandwiches and SPF of varying degrees (and aloe!); and pile into a car for a brisk jaunt to the shore. You're living your best life with brand-new sunglasses, a swimsuit that makes you feel glam, and that huge beach towel your mom got you at Costco that is *not* glam but is so comfy it almost feels like a blanket, and you and your friends are belting out old-school Britney Spears and new-school Carly Rae Jepsen like you're eighteen again and/or starring in a Disney Channel Original Movie.

In the spirit of full honesty, it might not be perfect: your friend's hat could fly off and the beach might be overrun with children, but you *will* find a spot, and you *will* have a great time, and you *will* find yourself and all your friends in the ocean, jumping through the waves and feeling more refreshed than you've felt in ages. And going home, you'll be exhausted in that perfect way that comes with spending the day outdoors and in the sun; and tonight, you're going to sleep like a baby. You are absolutely doing summer right.

FALL ACTIVITY: HAUNTED HOUSE TOGETHER VERSUS PUMPKIN PATCH WITH YOUR DOG

- *If You're in a Relationship:* Why lie: this will inevitably end in tears. As an unashamed and unrepentant scaredy-cat, a haunted house sounds to me like the absolute worst fall activity that one could partake in, but people like what they like, and in the words of country songstress Kacey Musgraves, "follow your arrow wherever it points," even if it points directly into the mouth of hell.

If you force someone who hates haunted houses to go, no, they will *not* decide they suddenly like it, and no, despite your teenaged fantasies, clutching your partner's arm is not romantic for either partner! The scared person will be terrified, and the not-scared person will end up with a viciously bruised arm and probably a bruised eardrum from the horrified screeches of their partner. Even worse is if the not-scared person is unsympathetic about the terror the scared person is undergoing. Yes, we scared people understand that nothing about it is real, and yes, we expect people to jump out at us, but we Simply! Don't! Like! It! Sorry, our brains have been evolutionarily hardwired to be prepared for danger. We know that we will absolutely be the first to die in a zombie apocalypse! We can't help these things, they just *are*!

Look, the solution here is simple: if someone likes haunted houses, they should go with people who also enjoy them. Everyone involved (and not involved!) will have so much more fun that way.

- *If You're Single:* You know what's decidedly *not* scary and is actually just freaking adorable? Going to a pumpkin patch—with your dog. Hop in the car with your favorite furry friend (borrowing one from a human friend is also acceptable, and I *suppose* the human friend can come along, although that's not the point of this scenario) and head out to a local pumpkin patch of choice (make sure you call ahead to confirm they will allow your esteemed companion). Once there, grab a roasted corn on the cob and let your doggo follow their nose wherever it points. Snap some pics of pup among the pumpkins; show the people in relationships how a Charlie Brown and Snoopy face cutout picture *should* look, thanks; and if you're feeling brave, venture into the corn maze. Make sure you pick up after your pet and know how much walking they can handle (especially the little pups!), and bask in a fight- (and fright-!) free afternoon. You've both earned it!

WINTER ACTIVITY: ICE-SKATING TOGETHER
VERSUS GINGERBREAD HOUSE–MAKING WITH FAMILY

- *If You're in a Relationship:* Whether you live in a big city, a chill suburb, or a rural town, my guess would be that you live near, have access to, or at least have heard of a temporary man-made ice-skating rink for the holiday season being created for—God, I don't know, festive cheer? A moneymaking Ponzi scheme? Whatever you call taking the money of unsuspecting patrons in exchange for a couple hours of absolute agony on your ankles, soles, and nerves. Many of us who are able have done and endured this "time-honored tradition," this picturesque, romanticized form of exercise/torture, and whether or not we ended up enjoying it or sulking at a nearby hot-chocolate stand, we've all witnessed the lovey-dovey couples who swarm the place like hipsters at a new farm-to-table restaurant.

There are many dangers at an ice-skating rink, including wild, zooming children; incredibly uncoordinated amateurs; and overconfident "I took skating lessons for three months ten years ago" show-offs, etc., but none are more dangerous or exasperating than That Couple, who are simultaneously clinging to both the rink edge and each other while trying to take the ideal photo and not fall down. Equally horrifying is that, if they happen to be a straight couple, the man then may try to skate backward while clasping hands with the woman while he "teaches" her how to skate, but in reality he is just as terrible as she is. Being god-awful at something as difficult as ice-skating isn't a crime, but it becomes one when you both put other people unnecessarily at risk *and* are incredibly annoying/into PDA! Do everyone a favor, and just sign up for couples' ice-skating lessons.

- *If You're Single:* Holidays can be rough, and many times being with certain family members only makes it worse instead of better. Like, for the love of God, Uncle Ted, stop pretending you're a political pundit. That said, whoever *you* consider to be family can, and should, partake in gingerbread house–making with you.

Set the mood by wearing your favorite cozy (but okay-to-get-wrecked) sweater, turning on your favorite Christmas (or anti-Christmas) music, and making a huge batch of mulled wine. If you're the host, all the better, because you can be festive, spend quality time with people you actually enjoy, *and* not have to go anywhere. It's a foolproof plan. Bonus points if you buy a village's worth of gingerbread house kits from Michaels or Trader Joe's and you turn it into a (very fun, very lighthearted—you're not an idiot, no need to tempt fate) contest.

And if you're like, "Oh, no, I'm not artistic or good at these things at all," let me be frank: no one cares. Remember those days in school when you would slather together frosting and graham crackers around washed-out milk cartons your teachers made you collect the month before? Everyone's house was terrible and *that's how it should be.* The blessedly beautiful thing about gingerbread houses is that there's no "coloring inside the lines" mentality here, no neat stitches or any actual skills necessary. Go hog wild with the Skittles and gumdrops; eat half the frosting and use the other half to write "Grinches Only" on the side of your dilapidated-looking roof; or get a huge bag of shredded dried coconut, toss half of it onto your house, and declare it a snowed-in cabin in the woods. It's all Art™!

For years boomers told us, as they handed us our Participation trophies (ones they made, by the way, not ones that we asked for), that everyone is talented in their own way, that everyone is *special*. Not everyone can hit a ball with a bat or run very fast or sing very well, but that's okay! Everyone is good at something, and it's *just fine* if you haven't figured out your talent yet.

As a kid, I believed adults who told me that stuff, and then I grew up and realized it was (well-meaning, but misguided) crap. Now, perhaps, I'm realizing that maybe boomers weren't too far off base, after all. Perhaps we do have all our own talents; there just aren't the proper outlets to showcase and recognize them all properly.

Well, if I were in charge, I would change that, at least a little bit. For instance, forget Olympics that are purely athletic-based. *Boring.* Don't we have enough sports, like, all the time? What about showcasing the talents of the Average Joe, the Everyman (should I call them Jolympics? No? I'll workshop it . . .). Granted, I can't promise it would be super exciting to watch, but hey, I would also bring back those cute little trophies, and that's something, right?

Categories would include:

- Longest Dating App Message-Convo that Never Led to a Date IRL
- Most Elaborately Constructed Fantasy in the Shower
- How Many Relatives at a Family Reunion Tried to Set You Up with Their Neighbor/Acquaintance
- How Many Days You Can Go Without Washing Your Hair (but It Still Looks Acceptable in Public) Post-Breakup
- How Many Meals You Can Make This Chinese Take-out Last
- Most Random Places You Can Fall Asleep
- Longest Netflix Binge Period
- Most Conspicuous Irish Exit at an Engagement Party
- How Many of Your Tinder Matches Are Actually Just Hunting for a Third in a Threesome
- Lasts the Longest When Talking to Meddling Relatives
- Longest Nap in a Bed All by Yourself
- Number of Dates It Takes for the Bartender at Your Designated "First Date Bar" to Recognize You on Sight

A LIST OF PLACES YOU CAN TRAVEL TO
SINCE YOU'RE SINGLE AND CHILDLESS

Sometimes even Singles can catch a break and get away from the masses and forced mingling, and there's no arena in which Singles shine more than vacationing. This is when you absolutely do not want a family, let alone a significant other, to appease while you take advantage of your precious time away! So where are the best places to go as a single person sans children?

- **Italy:** Have you ever been to a local Olive Garden and seen a grubby toddler in a sticky high chair try to eat pasta with their hands? You may try to avoid looking directly into the intense and often soulless eyes of children when at all possible, but this is an experience that should be viewed at least once—it's more revolting than any *Saw* movie. The carnage that is marinara sauce and chunks of tomato, splattered on every square inch of that toddler's body (and the high chair, and the floor, and probably the wall closest to them), is one that you won't be able to forget anytime soon. That said, could you imagine taking one of those mini pasta demons to *Italy* with you? You should be able to eat your perfectly al dente pasta in peace, dammit! We want our Italian vacation to be *Lady and the Tramp,* not *Lady and the Tramp II: Scamp's Adventure* (essentially the same movie, but with their children). Travel Tip: Use your savings to buy a ticket to Italy, rather than a new car seat, and eat three bowls of pasta per day in perfect silence.

- **The United Kingdom:** What do people in the United Kingdom even *do* besides drink in pubs, watch soccer ("footie") matches (also alcohol-soaked), and drink tea? Who can honestly say (Taylor Swift, help an American girl out?), but could you imagine children liking any of those things? Halfway through the soccer game the kid would need, like, a nap, or a sandwich, or just complain about when the game would be over. It's like, "Excuse me, small human, do you not think that I, too, would not like a nap or a sandwich at this time??" And it's doubtful that people traveling with children ever get any naps at all. The horror! Travel Tip: In your singledom, go to the UK, live your best Bridget Jones wine-filled life, and nap every day from 3 to 5 p.m. before enjoying London's best nightlife.

- **Hawaii:** Hear me out—many, many people vacation in Hawaii with their families. It's also likely that many of them actually enjoy said vacations and love bringing their children along! But consider instead: not. Rather than being woken up at 6 a.m. to the sight of duck-themed floaties being shoved in your face as their tiny owners screech to go to the beach, you can actually sleep in on your vacation! A concept! Beach time can be spent lounging in a chair, reading the latest "dad thriller" and/or "mom romance" without actually being a dad or mom! You can devote your full attention to your novel/mai tai/tanning regimen, and not have to play lifeguard/sand castle mediator/toy rescuer. Travel Tip: Go to a beach where you can truly pretend you're on a deserted island, away from the masses.

- **Anywhere:** Literally anywhere. The world is your oyster! There are definitely parts of the world in which it's good to travel with someone else, but despite adhering to the beloved kindergarten tradition of the "buddy system," said buddy doesn't actually need to be in kindergarten! You can do a walkabout of the Rockies, *Wild*-style; brave the peaks of Peru and see Machu Picchu; stay up all night karaoke'ing and then spa'ing in Korea; go on a Mexican cruise (heavy on the tequila); tour a Kenyan wildlife sanctuary; drink wine on the French Riviera; and even, despite what some haters say, take yourself on a Disneyland/Disney World vacation! Granted, there will be *so many children* there, but there's something perversely gleeful about being able to Fast Pass your heart out, get drunk at Epcot, and go back for more, all while staring into the faces of miserable, exhausted parents everywhere and being able to thank your lucky stars that their fate isn't yours. Travel Tip: Treat yo'self, and *only* yo'self.

PATRON SAINTS OF SINGLE PEOPLE, BOTH REAL AND FICTIONAL

It's a tough world out there, and it's really only natural that sometimes we mere mortals turn to divine intervention/ salvation for help and guidance in the messes we've made of our lives.

Sometimes praying to the Big Guy doesn't quite cut it, though: specificity and solidarity are required, which is where the Patron Saints of Single People come in. Spanning through real-life figures and pop-culture icons (both real and fictional), while not all of them are necessarily single, they all have Been There and can provide excellent guidance and comfort in times of trouble.

LIZ LEMON
Patron Saint of the Socially Awkward

Oh, Liz. For seven seasons of *30 Rock*, her boss Jack Donaghy, and many people around her, would despair of her and her utter lack and/or blatant disregard of social cues and boundaries. As she once famously said, "Ain't no party like a Liz Lemon party because a Liz Lemon party is *mandatory*!" She also once welcomed it when people booed her because she knew she was "right." To be honest, it's shocking she even bothered attending any parties at all, since everyone knows she'd rather be at home "working on her night cheese." Liz is (and I say this with love) a gross little gremlin of a woman who'd rather eat cheesy blasters with her mouth full than be a functional human being. And yet, Liz is all of us, at least some small part of us that we try to repress for the sake of humanity and social niceties, something Liz never bothered getting the hang of because she simply didn't care. But I'm here to say that she is, and you are, valid. Light a candle for Liz when you have to go to some social event you really don't want to attend and are mentally and emotionally not feeling it. I'm not saying stuff some cheesy blasters in your mouth so you don't have to talk all night, but fortify yourself in the armor of someone like Liz who is socially awkward and yet doesn't care at all. In its own weird way, that's confidence. Mantra: "Blerg." (Repeat in the style of *Om.*)

LESLIE KNOPE

Patron Saint of Single-Minded Determination

Leslie Knope has one goal: to be a public servant in the government and be the best she can be. She takes a lot of twists and turns during the entirety of *Parks and Recreation*, with various setbacks both personal and professional, but she never loses sight of her goal, and she never gives up. Even some of her setbacks turn into opportunities. Light a candle for Leslie when you're feeling like things professionally might seem hopeless and you need some optimism for the short term so you can plan for the long term anew. Mantra: "Do it. Fierce. Power."

AMY SANTIAGO
Patron Saint of Working the System

Perhaps less well-known than other Mike Schur–created TV heroines, Amy Santiago of *Brooklyn Nine-Nine* is no less formidable for it. A police sergeant, she's like the Cuban American version of Hermione Granger, if Hermione Granger traded in her wand for a gun and taser, that is. An unapologetic "nerd," as her love interest would call her, Amy is all about following the rules, or at least knowing them all so she can bend them to her will, if the situation calls. Ask for Amy's guidance when you need the reminder that while there are many systems in this trash fire of a world that should be burnt to the ground and rebuilt, unfortunately, for now, you have to work within them to get things done. Mantra: "Bureaucracy is a beautiful puzzle waiting to be cracked."

ELLE WOODS
Patron Saint of Personal Evolution

When the flawless classic film *Legally Blonde* begins, Elle Woods is content to be known as Delta Nu's president and her boyfriend Warner's future trophy wife. When he unceremoniously dumps her for someone "less of a Marilyn [Monroe] and more of a Jackie [Kennedy]," Elle's dreams shift to become more in line with what she thinks Warner wants. As we all know, over the course of the movie her dreams and ambitions evolve to be what *she* wants, which is entirely different from where she began. Think of Saint Elle when you feel stuck and bored with your life. Applicable to both career and fashion choices, remember to take risks and be open-minded if you want to truly change and evolve. Mantra: "Trust me, I can handle anything."

CRISTINA YANG

Patron Saint of Unrepentant Ambition

Cristina Yang of *Grey's Anatomy* is a smart-mouthed, loyal-as-hell, excellent surgeon whose glorious mane of curly hair is almost as big as her genius brain. Like Leslie Knope, Cristina Yang knows exactly what she wants and is determined to get there at all costs and setbacks, even if they're difficult. When her on-again, off-again husband and lover Owen Hunt wants to have children, which Cristina has never wanted, Cristina knows that it would change everything, especially her goals. No matter how much she loves Owen, she stands firm in her decision, and ultimately chooses her career over him. Turn to Cristina Yang when someone wants you to waver on something you feel strongly about, especially if it's your goals and dreams, and you need the strength to push back and stand firm. Mantra: "Pretty good is not good enough. I wanna be great."

PHRYNE FISHER

Patron Saint of Rule-Breaking

If you've never heard of or watched *Miss Fisher's Murder Mysteries*, I can say with 100 percent certainty that you're missing out. Set in 1920s Australia and based on a popular series of murder-mystery books, this TV series follows Phryne Fisher, a spitfire "lady detective" who defies typical convention by refusing to be a proper genteel spinster, and instead runs around Melbourne solving murders while brandishing her own golden gun and taking many (*many*) lovers. Phryne tosses her sleek-black-bobbed head at the expectations that others constantly try to put on her, breaking rules like she breaks hearts. Pray to Phryne when you're in the mood to defy outdated societal conventions (like the patriarchy!) and need the confidence and strength to do so. Mantra: "I dance to no one's tune."

SAMANTHA JONES

Patron Saint of Unashamed Sexual Energy

Even if you've never watched *Sex and the City*, it was basically a given that you had to know if you were a "Carrie, Samantha, Charlotte, or Miranda." In my experience, very few people proudly proclaimed they were a Samantha, which is a bit of a shame, because in my opinion Samantha is a pretty awesome person to be. While she was more than just her sexcapades, there's no denying that Samantha Jones was, first and foremost, portrayed as a sexual creature. Not only was she unashamed of her own desires, she was fearless in voicing them, both to her sexual partners in the boudoir and to her friends outside of it. She was a woman who knew exactly what she liked and had no trouble voicing it—you could even call her the poster child for explicit and enthusiastic consent on TV. Call upon Samantha when you find yourself in need of that sexual confidence in your life. Mantra: "I am done with great love, now I'm back to great lovers."

BEYONCÉ
Patron Saint of Planning

What makes Beyoncé so good at what she does (besides being incredibly talented and driven) is her excellent creative vision, her care and purpose in everything she does, her eye for the details in her performances, and her meticulous planning of them. She can take massive projects that seem overwhelming and make them look flawless. If you've ever seen the Beychella documentary, you've had the behind-the-scenes look at what it took to pull off her Coachella takeover and know that she's a woman who knows all angles of her craft and excels at it. Pray to Bey when you're in the weeds with a tough project and need the stamina to see it through or the creativity to look at it from another angle. Mantra: "It's not about perfection. It's about purpose."

ARIANA GRANDE
Patron Saint of Moving On

I mean, is this one really that big of a surprise? That girl has had so many ups and downs, I'm sure you know all of them, and a good chunk have involved her romantic partners. I've heard people say that a failed relationship feels like they wasted time on someone, and while it's certainly true that people can be in relationships that they should've left sooner, it doesn't mean that just because a relationship fails it was a waste of time. Just like mistakes, there are lessons to be learned in every relationship, and no one knows that more than Ari. She is absolutely the person to turn to after a terrible breakup, no matter what stage you're in; she will advocate patience and kindness to yourself and magnanimity to your exes. Mantra: "Thank you, next."

SHONDA RHIMES
Patron Saint of Saying Yes

The creator of iconic shows like *Grey's Anatomy*, *Scandal*, *How to Get Away with Murder*, etc., the Empress of Shondaland didn't get to where she is by playing it safe and never taking risks. She obviously covered that in her book *Year of Yes*, but the point of her book wasn't necessarily about saying "yes" to everything, it was about doing what was best for yourself to live the best life you could, whether that meant taking care of your own needs and interests or taking risks. So say a little prayer to Shonda if what you need is the confidence and strength to build the best life you can. Mantra: "Be brave. Be amazing. Be worthy."

CARRIE FISHER
Patron Saint of Bravery and Badassery

Perhaps the only woman more formidable and strong than the ass-kicking, Empire-destroying, take-no-nonsense Princess Leia is the woman who played her, Carrie Fisher (RIP,

MAY SPACE MOM REST IN PEACE, WE LOVE YOU, SPACE MOM. SO TRAGIC HOW SHE DIED IN THE MOONLIGHT, STRANGLED BY HER OWN BRA). Carrie Fisher always spoke her mind, and was incredibly open about her struggles with addiction and mental health, long before people became more open with the subjects. In addition to being an all-around badass, she took no shit from anyone. One time when she found out a producer was harassing her friend, she sent him a severed cow tongue in a box as a warning. What's not to love! Neither Princess Leia nor Carrie Fisher ever shied away from anything, no matter how tough. Call on Carrie when you need to be brave, and, like the Force, she'll guide you! Mantra: "Stay afraid, but do it anyway."

MAXINE WATERS
Patron Saint of Reclaiming Time

It was the line heard 'round the internet when, in 2017 during a House Committee on Financial Services meeting, Congresswoman Maxine Waters stonily and succinctly said to then–Treasury Secretary Steven Mnuchin that she would be "reclaiming [her] time" after his attempts to stall her questioning. It was a phrase that many people identified with, whether it was specific to men mansplaining to women or meetings that could be emails. Make entreaties to Maxine when you need to do the tough thing and reclaim your time, and not just from your enemies, but from people who are important to you, like your friends, family, or significant others. It's important to set and enforce boundaries for your own health, and Maxine will give you the strength to do it. Mantra: "Do what your heart and soul tell you to do."

MEGAN RAPINOE
Patron Saint of Demanding More

When Megan Rapinoe helped lead the US Women's Soccer team to victory at the 2019 World Cup, she obviously (and awesomely) celebrated her and her team's well-deserved win, but she also took that time with her newfound popularity and elevated platform to call out the huge pay disparity between herself and her male counterparts. She and her team sued the US Soccer Federation for equal pay, and she refused to back down on that or any of her other strong-willed opinions. Summon your inner Soccer Goddess when you need to demand more—whether it's also a pay raise, a promotion, or just to be treated better by those around you. If you need to have your voice be heard, the spirit of Megan is the exact right one to count on. Mantra: "Do what you can. Do what you have to do."

KRIS JENNER
Patron Saint of Cunning Schemes

No matter what you think of the Kardashian Klan or their matriarch, one thing can't be denied: the devil works hard, but Kris Jenner works harder. Kris took what was a humiliating, awful moment for her daughter, whose privacy was invaded via sex tape, and somehow, a decade or so later, has a multichild, multibillion-dollar empire to show for it. She's the Best-Known Momager in the entire world (and rightly so) and always has a few (dozen) tricks up her sleeves and schemes cooking away. Shakespeare said that all the world's a stage, but Kris Jenner knows it's actually a chessboard, and she's somehow purchased every single piece on it, able to move each one at her will. Kall on Kris (hmmm, do I smell a future spin-off series in which Kris Jenner gives advice? Yes?!) when you need to be at your absolute best, when you need to scheme and plot and plan and get things done, one way or another. To be fair, I wouldn't recommend utilizing Kris *too* often, but sometimes she's just the woman to get things done. Mantra: "Be ready to pivot on a dime."

IX.

The Brochure

Once upon a time, I created a (fake!) brochure to hand out at my cousin's wedding. It covered FAQs about my job and life in NYC, and it included reasons as to why I was single, all of which were true to me and my life. When I tweeted it out, multiple people asked if I could make a brochure for them. While I can't do that, I can give you the template to make your own.

WHO'S THAT GIRL: CREATE YOUR OWN BROCHURE

It can be absolutely nerve-racking in many ways when you're single and forced to mingle, and you have to do it at an event with people you haven't seen in a really long time. You've probably changed a lot, they've probably changed a lot, and you're inevitably prepping yourself to answer the same basic (yet somehow also invasive) questions over and over again.

You're a polite, reasonable person and you understand that this is the inherent nature of the little evil known as "small talk," but knowing that doesn't necessarily remove the anxiety you might feel over it.

Wouldn't it be easier, you think to yourself, if you could just give everyone some kind of FAQ sheet like the kind you devour every time your iPhone starts acting up again? It would, and while that still isn't a socially acceptable thing to actually do, it's fun to dream (or at the very least, plan/think about your answers so you're not just spewing out incoherent sentences only to obsess about them for the next several days).

Here's a template to get you started, although obviously, in the words of Amy Poehler in *Baby Mama*, "I don't know your life!" So adjust as needed.

JOB FAQs

What do you do again?
My advice: keep it as short and simple as possible, because you know that they're only asking to be polite and will inevitably forget your answer five minutes after you walk away from them/ after the second glass of wine hits their bloodstream.

Doesn't it have to do with [insert general misconception about your profession here]?
Before you make an Arthur-clenched-fist, take a deep breath and a sip of whatever you're drinking, alcoholic or not, before you answer. You feel like you answer this question constantly, and you do, but it is too early in the night to lose it now. Deep breaths!

Your mom recently told me that [mangled version of a story that you told your mom several months ago]. Is this true?
If your mom passive-aggressively bugs you as to why you don't call often, make sure you use this story as an example.

My son/daughter/niece/next-door neighbor is interested in what you do. Can I give them your number so they can call you and ask about your job?
Listen, it's up to you to figure out how generous you want to be here. Maybe an email would be better, because lord knows the last thing you want is to be stuck on the phone as you reiterate these exact same answers to a total stranger for forty-five minutes.

LIVING FAQs

How's living in [city]?
What else can you say besides "great!" here? If you hate it, I suppose you could be honest, but inevitably you know what the follow-up question is going to be, and do you really want to give the questioner the satisfaction of confirming all of their prejudices against your home-away-from-home? Out of spite, the only correct answer here is: absolutely not.

I've heard that living in [city] is so [insert negative stereotype here]. How do you stand it?
Whew, doesn't that get your blood boiling! You can just tell that if someone phrases a question like this, they're fishing for a specific answer, and you're not going to give it to them! Feel free to lie through your teeth here if you need to, just to not give them the satisfaction.

Where do you live again? What landmark are you by?
Honestly, again, you could make up a neighborhood and landmark, particularly if this person isn't familiar with the area in which you live. I promise they won't remember at all, so who cares.

Do you ever see [insert tourist trap/ landmark here]?
We all know the answer is: of course not.

We were just there several years ago. If we're ever in the area again, we should catch up!
Your generosity is up to you, but there's nothing wrong with being polite and noncommittal!

The Prototype

L E F T Include work details here… Because what you do is apparently correlated to your single status.

←

 **MIDDLE** ←

Include fun pic here… To remind those nonsingle people what they're missing out on.

Include your location here… Since where you live is definitely better than dragging yourself to yet another event. **R I G H T**

→

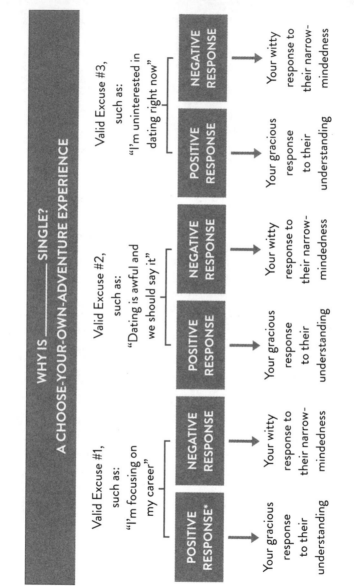

WHY IS _____ SINGLE?
A CHOOSE-YOUR-OWN-ADVENTURE EXPERIENCE

Valid Excuse #1, such as: "I'm focusing on my career"

POSITIVE RESPONSE*	NEGATIVE RESPONSE
Your gracious response to their understanding	Your witty response to their narrow-mindedness

Valid Excuse #2, such as: "Dating is awful and we should say it"

POSITIVE RESPONSE	NEGATIVE RESPONSE
Your gracious response to their understanding	Your witty response to their narrow-mindedness

Valid Excuse #3, such as: "I'm uninterested in dating right now"

POSITIVE RESPONSE	NEGATIVE RESPONSE
Your gracious response to their understanding	Your witty response to their narrow-mindedness

*You know your respective Aunt Carol better than I do, so only you can guess what she'll say!

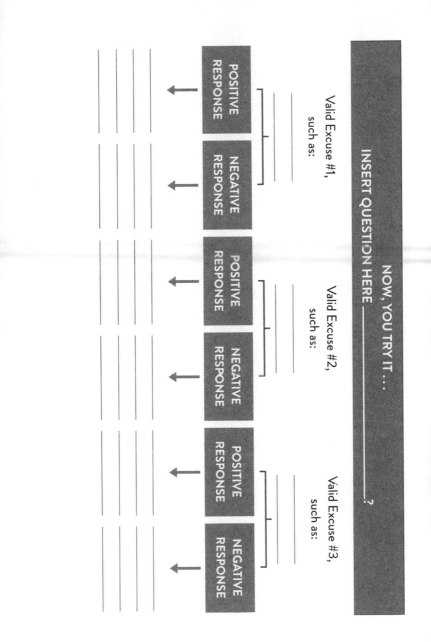

NOW, YOU TRY IT . . .

INSERT QUESTION HERE _____?

Valid Excuse #1,
such as:

POSITIVE RESPONSE

NEGATIVE RESPONSE

Valid Excuse #2,
such as:

POSITIVE RESPONSE

NEGATIVE RESPONSE

Valid Excuse #3,
such as:

POSITIVE RESPONSE

NEGATIVE RESPONSE

Acknowledgments

A single person may be, well, *single*, but even they are no island, and this particular single person was fortunate enough to have nearly an entire country's worth of people who helped create this book, both logistically and emotionally.

First and foremost, I must thank the two other members of the triumvirate of this book: my agent, Jon Michael Darga, and my editor, Lara Jones. When my brochure tweet went viral, I was pretty content to passively run out my twenty seconds of fame, but they were the ones who thought I had something special on my hands and encouraged me to turn it into a book. I'll always fondly treasure the memories of our impromptu initial FaceTime brainstorming sessions as we frantically typed ideas into a shared Google doc as fast as our mouths moved. People warn you about doing business with your friends, but it's probably because most people don't have friends and partners like these two. There's no one else I would want to have at my side for this process, which you've made so easy and smooth with your brilliance and dedication. Thank you to the entire team at Atria; working with you all has been phenomenal. I've learned so much and have been consistently impressed with your commitment. The executive team of publisher Libby McGuire, associate publisher Suzanne Donahue, editorial director Lindsay Sagnette, and director of integrated marketing Kristin Fassler have been so supportive. The dynamic duo of publicist Megan Rudloff and marketing manager Isabel DaSilva are truly a dream team. Books that read so perfectly and are laid out so nicely don't come out of thin air: this particular book came from the managing editorial and production teams consisting of managing editor Paige Lytle, assistant managing editor Jessie McNeil, and production manager Jim Thiel. And because people really do judge a book by its cover, I could not be more thankful that I had art director James Iacobelli and associate art director Laywan Kwan making sure I had the most beautiful package (inside and out!) possible, courtesy of illustrator Ella Laytham and interior designer Dana Sloan. I especially appreciated their patience when I kept making cover adjustments—thanks for indulging this perfectionist!

Without the support of the abovementioned publishing team, this book would be nothing, but without the support of my family and friends, *I* would be nothing.

To my parents, Mike and Chris Croce, thank you for always letting me be myself, for guiding me but never stifling me, even though I'm sure there were many, *many* times you pondered how on earth could you have possibly produced me because we're all so different from one another. I'm pretty sure I wouldn't be so self-actualized and well-adjusted if it weren't for you always giving me a safe space to grow and learn and figure out who I was for myself.

To my brothers, John and Ryan, please know that I'm forever grateful that I'm a single person but not a single child, no matter what kind of "No John/Ryan Allowed" signs I used to tape to my bedroom door. I'm so proud to be your big sister. Thanks for always keeping me humble, but having my back, anyway.

To my grandparents, Mel and Ellen Char, thank you both for truly being my biggest fans. Grandpa, you always believed I would write and publish a book more than I believed it myself, and, despite my sizable ego, that unwavering belief helped me more than I could say. Grandma, I don't think there's a better cheerleader than you out there—who else would follow along with their granddaughter's tweets, forward her tiny letter to friends, and shamelessly brag about her at every opportunity to every person she meets?

And, because I'm sure people are wondering, I do not literally have an Aunt Carol. Instead, I'm lucky enough to have a delightful extended family of many uncles, aunties, and cousins. Particular thanks to the always-supportive Char, Johnson, and Ryser families.

To all of my Macmillan Children's coworkers, who the brochure was inspired by, I've so appreciated your unwavering excitement and support. I especially want to thank the Scheme Team: Katie Halata, Kristen Luby, and Cierra Bland. Teamwork really does make the scheme dream work. And Katie has been the absolute best momager a girl could ask for—sorry, Kardashian and Jenner kids, you can't have her! Single life is so sweet when you have friends like mine. What gems you all are! Thank you to the "Storehouse Squad": Tiara Kittrell, Grace Rosean, Heather Job, Rachel Murray, Teresa Ferraiolo, Caitlin Crocker, Jessica Anderson, and Mark Podesta. I wouldn't have lasted all these years in NYC without you, and I wouldn't ever want to try. Thank you to Emily Weaver, my near-birthday twin and fellow Scorpio: it's

ACKNOWLEDGMENTS

been an honor to grow up in our twenties together, through college and across the country, and I'm sure our thirties will be equally spectacular (but with less mimosas). And thank you to: Felicia Deng, Michael Diana, Emily DuVal, Aimee Fleck, Brieana Garcia, Chelsea Greensitt, Caitlin Kidder, Tara Kumar, Danielle Lucero, Summer Ogata, Will Rhino, Alexis Sattler, Katie Schmidt, and Jenn Tapler. Near or far, I am so fortunate to have you all in my life.

Jon and Lara, I know I've already thanked you two, but you were my friends before you were my agent and editor, and I can do what I want here (within word count), so I'm thanking you again as my friends. Jon Darga, how lucky am I that we found each other in this simulation: the Cristina Yang to my Cristina Yang. I'm honored to be a part of such an incredibly powerful friendship, one that neither Jarrís nor distance can touch. I can't wait to see what universes we create and what else we'll achieve. Lara Jones, most people *wish* that their friendships/roommate-ships were as solid as ours, and filled with as much laughter, made-up songs, and Miss Fisher, and why wouldn't they? From the 'Schwick to South Slope, I couldn't ask for a better platonic wife-4-life. Again: thank you, thank you, thank you to you both, the Birdo and Waluigi, respectively, to my Rosalina. A match made in both Mario Kart and real-world heaven.

Completely pivoting, I want to thank my enemies and haters, because sometimes forgiveness is overrated and spite can be a very productive motivator when working toward your dreams. I won't name names because they're not worth the word count, but I would particularly like to recognize a former social studies teacher who spent one lesson telling my class

ACKNOWLEDGMENTS

that we would never change the world and that our names would all be forgotten in a hundred years. Well, sir, this book might not make me generationally famous, but it—and subsequently my name—are going into the Library of Congress, where *you* certainly won't be. (*My* lesson to you: a Scorpio never forgets.)

(That said, genuinely, thank you to the many teachers and librarians I had who were wonderful and encouraging. I was extremely lucky in that the good ones outweighed the bad.)

My inner conscience, which tends to sound like my parents, is telling me to wrap this up (Mom) and on a positive note (Dad), so I'll say lastly, thank you to everyone who related to, liked, retweeted, and commented on that infamous brochure tweet. It's wild to think about, but truly, none of this would've happened without you scrolling and tapping on that little heart. I little-heart you, too.

About the Author

MELISSA CROCE is a Pacific Northwest native who left her beloved rainy region behind to work in children's publishing in New York. When she's not working, she can be found sleeping, reading tarot cards, watching hockey games, and spending way too much time on the internet, which is how *Single and Forced to Mingle* initially came to be. You can find her on Twitter @MelissaCroce.

Notes

For All Your Single-Life Rants and Raves

Notes

Notes